*Everyman, I will go with thee,
and be thy guide*

D0873644

THE EVERYMAN
LIBRARY

The Everyman Library was founded by J. M. Dent
in 1906. He chose the name Everyman because he wanted
to make available the best books ever written in every
field to the greatest number of people at the cheapest possible
price. He began with Boswell's 'Life of Johnson';
his one-thousandth title was Aristotle's 'Metaphysics',
by which time sales exceeded forty million.

Today Everyman paperbacks remain true to
J. M. Dent's aims and high standards, with a wide range
of titles at affordable prices in editions which address
the needs of today's readers. Each new text is reset to give
a clear, elegant page and to incorporate the latest thinking
and scholarship. Each book carries the pilgrim logo,
the character in 'Everyman', a medieval mystery play,
a proud link between Everyman
past and present.

VICTORIAN
WOMEN POETS
1830–1901

AN ANTHOLOGY

Edited by
JENNIFER BREEN
University of North London

EVERYMAN
J. M. DENT · LONDON
CHARLES E. TUTTLE
VERMONT

Introduction and Notes © Jennifer Breen 1994

This edition first published in Everyman in 1994

J. M. Dent
Orion Publishing Group
Orion House,
5 Upper St Martin's Lane,
London WC2H 9EA
and
Charles E. Tuttle Co. Inc.
28 South Main Street,
Rutland, Vermont 05701, USA

Typeset in Sabon by
CentraCet Limited, Cambridge
Printed in Great Britain by
The Guernsey Press Co. Ltd, Guernsey, C.I.

British Library Cataloguing-in-Publication Data
is available upon request.

ISBN 0 460 87457 8

CONTENTS

vi

viii

NOTES ON THE AUTHORS

ELIZABETH BARRETT BROWNING (1806–61) was born in
Durham, the eldest in a family of eight boys and three girls. She
was brought up on her father's estate, Hope End, near Ledbury
in Herefordshire. Her mother, Mary Barrett (née Graham-
Clarke), encouraged her writing when she was still a child, and
her father, Edward Moulton Barrett, organized and paid for the
publication of her first books of poems, *The Battle of Marathon*
(1820), and *An Essay on Mind with Other Poems* (1826).
Elizabeth learnt Greek and Latin with the tutor employed for
Edward (nicknamed 'Bro'), her eldest brother, until he went to
board at Charterhouse School in 1820 when she was fourteen.
Her strange malady, which began in 1821, and which Maggie
Lane diagnoses as a 'form of tuberculosis, susceptible to long
periods of remission but always present in the background and
liable to be brought on by nervous excitement: a real illness,
and the one from which she eventually died, but influenced by
her subconscious', commenced at about this time (Maggie Lane,
Literary Daughters (1989), Robert Hale, p. 82). Elizabeth
continued her studies herself in an informal way, especially from
1826 to 1832 when she worked as an amanuensis for the blind
Greek scholar, Hugh Stuart Boyd. Although Boyd was both
much older and married, she found him intellectually stimulat-
ing and companionable. After her mother's death in 1828, when
Elizabeth was twenty-two, her father became determined to
prevent his eldest daughter from marrying. In 1832, the Barrett
family were forced, because of financial losses, to move from
their Victorian mansion, Hope End, which her father had built
with profits from the sugar trade in the West Indies. They
eventually settled at Wimpole Street, London, where Elizabeth
led a secluded life as a poet and invalid. On one of her excursions
to Torquay in 1840, however, her brother Edward was drowned
when out in a boat. Elizabeth Barrett, who had insisted that
'Bro' remain with her at Torquay as a solace for the sudden

death in Jamaica of her second brother, Sam, felt that she had circumstantially brought about Bro's death. In 1844, Elizabeth Barrett published *Poems*, which were acclaimed, particularly by the poet Robert Browning, who wrote to her, and subsequently began to visit her, against her father's wishes, in 1845. In 1846, she eloped with Robert Browning to Italy; her father disinherited her, refusing always to see her, her husband or her son Pen, who was born in 1849. In Italy, Elizabeth Barrett Browning published a new collection, *Poems* (1850), which included *Sonnets from the Portuguese*, a semi-autobiographical series about her love for Robert Browning whose pet name for her was 'my little Portuguese'. Her subsequent works included *Casa Guidi Windows* (1851); a feminist verse-novel, *Aurora Leigh* (1856); *Poems before Congress* (1860), and her posthumous *Last Poems* (1861). Biographical information comes from *The Barretts at Hope End* (Elizabeth Berridge); *Robert Browning and Elizabeth Barrett* (Daniel Karlin); 'Elizabeth Barrett Browning' in *Literary Daughters* (Maggie Lane), pp. 75–101; and Dorothy Mermin's *Elizabeth Barrett Browning*. The poems from *Sonnets from the Portuguese* and the excerpt from *Aurora Leigh*, Book I, are taken from Elizabeth Barrett Browning, *Poetical Works* (F. G. Kenyon), pp. 318–9, 321–3, 327 and 352–66.

MATHILDE BLIND (1841–96), literary critic, dramatist and poet, was born Mathilde Cohen in Mannheim, Germany. She was brought to St John's Wood in London when she was eleven. Her stepfather, Karl Blind, a dissident, was forced to seek asylum with his wife, two stepchildren and two later children of his marriage with Mathilde's mother. Mathilde had begun her schooling in Belgium, and continued in several small private schools in London, but these experiences were so desultory that she claimed she had educated herself. She was well read in the Bible, Shakespeare and Goethe, as well as in the new theories about biological evolution which found expression in her epic poem, *The Ascent of Man* (1889). She deplored the lack of educational facilities for women, and was in favour of women's suffrage. A woman of independent means, in 1871 she established a home for herself separately from her parents. She tried various ways of employing her talents: she wrote verse, gave literary lectures and compiled several literary biographies, beginning with one on Shelley. Although some of these works, such as her long dramatic poems, received critical attention when first published, she never succeeded in making the mark on the Victorian age that she had hoped for. She was a friend of the Ford Madox Browns and the William Rossettis, and knew various celebrities such as Swinburne, Mazzini and Garibaldi. She travelled in England and on the Continent throughout her life, rarely settling long anywhere. In 1867 she published *Poems* under the pseudonym of Claude Lake, followed by, under her own name, *The Prophecy of Saint Oran and Other Poems* (1881), *Tarantella* (1885), *The Heather on Fire* (1886), *The Ascent of Man* (1889), *Dramas in Miniature* (1891), *Songs and Sonnets* (1893), and *Birds of Passage* (1895). Biographical information comes from Richard Garnett's 'Memoir' in *The Poetical Works of Mathilde Blind*, pp. 2–43. The text of 'Only A Smile' is taken from *Songs and Sonnets*, p. 61.

ANNE BRONTË (1820–49), poet and novelist, was the youngest of the six children of Patrick and Maria Brontë (née Branwell), who were all born and brought up in Haworth, Yorkshire. Patrick, the son of an Irish labourer, educated himself, became a schoolteacher at sixteen and at twenty-five entered St John's College, Cambridge, and became a clergyman, obtaining the living at Haworth in 1820. He wrote books of poetry and prose, as well as contributing to the local press. When his wife died eighteen months after their move to Haworth, her sister, Elizabeth Branwell, came to look after the Brontë children and to run the household. Patrick Brontë educated his five daughters along with his son, Branwell, but at one stage his daughters were sent to Cowan Bridge boarding-school. His two eldest daughters, Maria (b. 1814) and Elizabeth (b. 1815), became ill at Cowan Bridge and died of tuberculosis in 1824. Anne, Emily and Charlotte later attended Roe Head boarding-school, where Charlotte became a teacher for a time in 1835. An earlier minor event in the Brontë household—the purchase of a box of toy wooden soldiers by Patrick—stimulated a wealth of composition by the Brontë children: they made up stories about the soldiers and set them in the Kingdom of Glasstown. Later Emily and Anne created the world of Gondal in the South Pacific, while Charlotte and Branwell wrote about Angria, an imaginary kingdom set in Africa. Juliet Barker describes this work: 'The characters of Angria and Gondal quickly became mouthpieces for a positive flood of writing . . . Most of the writing was prose, but at suitable dramatic moments poetry was used to highlight emotional intensity and much of the Brontës' poetry belongs to this imaginary world rather than to personal experience.' Anne Brontë has attracted least attention from literary critics. She published her poems anonymously at first, along with her sisters, Charlotte and Emily, under the joint pseudonym of Currer [Charlotte], Ellis [Emily] and Acton [Anne] Bell, in the volume *Poems* (1846). Anne also wrote two novels, *Agnes Grey* (1847) and *The Tenant of Wildfell Hall* (1848). She died of tuberculosis in 1849. Biographical information comes from Tom Winnifrith's *The Brontës* and Rebecca Fraser's *Charlotte Brontë*. Texts are taken from *The Complete Poems of Anne Brontë*, pp. 3–4, 23–4, 25, 41–2, 65, 90–1 and 96–7.

CHARLOTTE BRONTË (1816–55), poet and novelist, was the third daughter of Patrick and Maria Brontë (see above). After her abortive attempts at teaching, and at founding a school, Charlotte acted as literary agent for herself and her two sisters when they paid Aylott and Jones to publish their *Poems* (1846). This edition of one thousand copies had sold only two in the first year, and by 1848 there were 961 remaining. Charlotte Brontë, disappointed with the sales figures for their poems, turned her attention to novel-writing, a genre in which she achieved considerable success. Her first novel, *Jane Eyre*, attracted a large readership and critical praise when it first appeared in 1847. Her subsequent novels, *Shirley* (1849) and *Villette* (1850), although they received a mixed reception from critics, sold well. An earlier manuscript of a novel, *The Professor* (1857), was published posthumously, because before her death publishers would not take it. At the age of thirty-eight, with some initial trepidation, Charlotte Brontë married the Reverend Arthur Bell Nicholls, her father's curate. She died eight months after her marriage when she was said to be pregnant, but the actual cause of her death has not been established. She probably died from exhaustion and dehydration brought about by excessive vomiting, but this final illness might have been complicated by tuberculosis. Her novels have received much critical attention, but her poems have been relatively neglected. Biographical information comes from Rebecca Fraser's *Charlotte Brontë*, and texts are taken from *The Poems of Charlotte Brontë*, pp. 49–51, 51–4, 59–61, 239–40 and 253.

EMILY BRONTË (1818–48), poet and novelist, was the fifth daughter born to Patrick and Maria Brontë, and was mainly educated at home by her father, although she spent some time in two boarding-schools (see above). In order to learn Continental methods of education so that they could later establish a school in Haworth, Emily and Charlotte travelled in 1842 to the Heger Pensionnat in Brussels, returning to Haworth at the end of the year. In 1846, Emily was at first reluctant to have her poems published alongside Charlotte's and Anne's, and, when she had agreed to publication, tried to excise references in them to her imaginary world of Gondal and its characters. Nevertheless, some of these references remain in these poems. Emily Brontë died of tuberculosis in 1848, after achieving fame with her novel *Wuthering Heights* (1847). Emily Brontë's novel and her poetry have up till now attracted more attention from literary critics than her sisters' writings have done. Biographical information comes from Edward Chitham's *A Life of Emily Brontë*; texts are taken from *The Complete Poems of Emily Jane Brontë*, pp. 1–3, 5–6, 7–8, 10–11, 17–18, 20–1 and 55.

MARY COLERIDGE (1861–1907), poet, novelist and essayist, was related to Samuel Taylor Coleridge, who was her father's great-uncle. Her father, Arthur Duke Coleridge, was a solicitor and Clerk of the Assize. He pursued artistic and literary interests through his friends, Tennyson, Browning, Ruskin, Millais and Holman Hunt, who frequently visited his home in London. Mary had a younger sister, Florence, but neither married, remaining at home throughout their lives. They were educated privately, and Mary became proficient at Hebrew, Latin, Greek and Italian. She read widely, including Tolstoy and Ibsen in translation. Mary flourished in a group of women friends, one of whom, Margaret Duckworth, married Henry Newbolt, with whom Mary became friendly, exchanging ideas for novels, and reading each other's poems. Although she had begun to write poetry at thirteen, her first volume of a few poems, *Fancy's Following*, was not published until 1896. She also wrote novels which were well received: *The Seven Sleepers of Ephesus* (1893); *The King with Two Faces* (1897); *The Fiery Dawn* (1901); *The*

Shadow on the Wall (1904); and *The Lady on the Drawing-Room Floor* (1906). Another novel, *Becq*, remained unfinished at her death. A collection of her essays, *Non Sequiteur*, appeared in 1900. Although she published all her prose works under her own name, her two books of poems appeared under the pseudonym of Anodos. The publication of her poems was encouraged by Robert Bridges, who helped her edit them for Mr Daniel, Provost of Worcester College, Oxford, who printed them on his private press. A year later, Laurence Binyon helped her to publish more of her poems, *Fancy's Guerdon*, in the 'Shilling Garland' series in which he had appeared. Subsequently, she had poems printed in an anthology, *The Garland*, and in the *Spectator* and the *Pilot*. In 1907, she died suddenly after an operation for appendicitis. Henry Newbolt edited *Poems by Mary E. Coleridge* (1907), a selection of 237 of her poems which was published posthumously. Biographical information comes from *The Collected Poems of Mary Coleridge*. Texts are taken from *Fancy's Following*, pp. 3, 4, 10–11, 18, 35, 39, 51, and from *Fancy's Guerdon*, pp. 25 and 27.

ELIZA COOK (1818–89), poet, essayist, and founder of a literary journal, *Eliza Cook's Journal* (1849–54), was the daughter of a tinsmith and brazier of Southwark, London. In 1827, the family moved to a smallholding in Horsham, Sussex. The last of eleven children, Eliza Cook educated herself, showing an outstanding talent for journalism. She published her first collection of poems, *Lays of A Wild Harp*, in 1835, and thereafter contributed verse to various periodicals. Her second volume, *Melaia and Other Poems* (1838) was very popular, as was her *Journal*, which was oriented towards a working-class readership. Illness prevented her continuing to edit this periodical, much of which she wrote herself, and selections of which she reprinted later in *Jottings from My Journal* (1860). She dressed in a practical manner, never married, and for a short time had a romantic friendship with the actress Charlotte Cushman, whom she courted with her own sonnets. Her poems ranged from ballads about the poor to sentimental quatrains about domestic scenes. Biographical information comes from *DNB* and Lillian Faderman's *Surpassing the Love of Men*, pp. 222–3. Text is reprinted from *Poems*, pp. 193–7.

GEORGE ELIOT (pseudonym of Mary Ann Evans) (1819–80) is best known as one of the leading novelists of her times, but her work as a translator, journalist and poet was also notable. Her small quantity of poetry has received scant attention from critics, but her sonnet sequence, 'Brother and Sister' (1869), with its naturalistic effects and emphasis on the unconscious nature of guilt and the possibilities of its resolution will appeal to readers today. These eleven sonnets encapsulate her childhood relationship with her older brother Isaac as she recalls it from the point of view of maturity. After George Eliot began to live openly with George Henry Lewes, a married man, Isaac abjured any relationship with his sister. He only contacted her again after Lewes died and she had married John Cross, a man much younger than herself. This break in her contact with her brother accounts for the elegiac tone of 'Brother and Sister'. Ironically, according to one of her biographers, Ruby Redinger, she found with Lewes the kind of companionship that she had enjoyed in childhood with Isaac. Redinger suggests that the composition of these sonnets helped George Eliot to resolve a temporary 'block' in her novel-writing. George Eliot wrote two books of poetry, *The Legend of Jubal and other Poems* (1874) and *The Spanish Gypsy: A Poem* (1886). Her novels are: *Scenes of Clerical Life*, 2 vols (1858); *Adam Bede*, 3 vols (1859); *The Mill on the Floss*, 3 vols (1860); *Silas Marner: the Weaver of Raveloe* (1861); *Romola*, 3 vols (1863); *Felix Holt: the Radical*, 3 vols (1866); *Middlemarch: A Study of Provincial Life*, 4 vols (1871); *Daniel Deronda*, 4 vols (1876); and *Impressions of Theophrastus*, 5 vols (1879). Biographical facts come from Ruby V. Redinger, *George Eliot* and Jennifer Uglow, *George Eliot*. Text of 'In A London Drawingroom' comes from *Collected Poems*, p. 41, and 'Brother and Sister' from *The Legend of Jubal and other Poems*, pp. 209–19.

MICHAEL FIELD is the pseudonym of two authors, Katharine Bradley (1846–1914) and Edith Cooper (1862–1913), who were aunt and niece. Katharine Bradley, who lived with her elder married sister, Emma Cooper (née Bradley), was sixteen when her sister gave birth to Edith. Edith was thus partly brought up by her Aunt Katharine. Katharine Bradley had strong maternal feelings towards her niece, in particular helping to educate her at home, especially in the Classics and in English poetry. In 1878, aunt and niece studied Classics and philosophy together at University College, Bristol. Katharine Bradley had already in 1875 published her first book of poetry, *The New Minnesinger*, under the neuter pseudonym of Arran Leigh. In 1881, Katharine and Edith published their first collaboration, *Bellerophon and other Poems*, using the names of Arran and Isla Leigh. Their poetry received little critical attention, and for their next work, a melodrama, *Callirrhoe* (1884), they chose the masculine name, Michael Field. *Callirrhoe* attracted favourable reviews until the fact that they were *two* women, aunt and niece, became known in literary circles, when their popularity waned. Because Bradley and Cooper shared private means, however, they continued writing poetic dramas and lyrics well into the twentieth century. They considered themselves to be part of the late nineteenth-century 'aesthetic' and 'decadent' movements, and some of their poems touch on lesbian eroticism (see, for example, 'Second Thoughts'). In their journal, *Work and Day*, edited by T. and D. C. Sturge Moore, which was published posthumously in 1933, Bradley and Cooper described their emotional intimacy and collaboration in writing as closer than that of Elizabeth Barrett and Robert Browning. But this comparison does not make much sense, since the Brownings did not grow up together, and when they met they were already highly individualistic established writers and not likely to begin writing collaboratively. These two women's poetic dramas under the pseudonym of 'Michael Field' include *The Father's Tragedy; William Rufus; Loyalty or Love* (1885); *Brutus Ultor* (1886); *Canute the Great* (1887); Cup of Water (1887); *The Tragic Mary* (1890); *A Question of Memory* (1893); *Attila, My Attila!* (1896); *Fair Rosamund* (1897); *The World at Auction* (1898); *Anna Ruina* (1899); and *Noontide Branches* (1899). Michael Field's volumes of poetry are *Long Ago* (1889); *Sight and Song* (1892); *Stephania; A Trialogue* (1892); and *Underneath the Bough* (1893). Biographical information comes from Mary Sturgeon, *Michael Field* and from Lillian Faderman, *Surpassing the Love of Men*, pp. 208–13. Text of 'Across a Gaudy Room' is reprinted from *Underneath the Bough*, pp. 88–9 and 'Second Thoughts' from *A Selection from the Poems of Michael Field*, p. 47.

DORA GREENWELL (1821–82), poet and essayist, was born into a landowning family and had four brothers. When she was twenty-seven, her father, through mismanagement, was forced to sell his property, Greenwell Ford, and Dora then lived with two of her brothers and later with her mother in Durham. After her mother's death in 1865, Dora Greenwell moved to London. Her books of poetry included *Poems* (1848), *Carmina Crucis* (1869), *The Soul's Legend* (1873) and *Camera Obscura* (1876). She also wrote secular and religious essays which were acclaimed in her day. One of the most interesting of these essays is 'Our Single Women', which appeared in the *North British Review* (February, 1862) and was subsequently collected in *Essays* (1866). In addition, she wrote religious books, including memoirs of religious men, such as the Quaker, John Woolman (1871). Biographical information comes from *DNB* and Henry Bett's *Dora Greenwell*. Text is reprinted from *Poems*, pp. 198–200.

JANET HAMILTON (née Thomson) (1795–1873), poet and essayist, was born in Shotts, Lanarkshire. Her father was variously a field labourer and shoemaker, and Hamilton taught herself to read and write. A spinner from childhood, she married her father's shoemaker assistant when she was only fourteen, and had ten children, seven of whom survived. She could read the Bible and children's 'halfpenny' books before she was five, and at eight she read Milton's *Paradise Lost*. Her subsequent reading in her village library was eclectic, including *Plutarch's Lives*, historical books, Robert Burns's poetry, and the *Spectator* and the *Rambler*. After her marriage, she worked on the spinning-wheel and tambour-frame. She kept up her reading, and taught her own children to read. Although she wrote a few poems as an adolescent, she did not begin to write publishable work until she was fifty-four, when she began to contribute to Cassell's *Working Man's Friend*. Her other works include *Poems and Essays of a Miscellaneous Character on Subjects of General Interest* (1863), from which the text is taken (pp. 37–41), and *Poems of Purpose and Sketches in Prose of Scottish Peasant Life and Character in Auld Lang Syne* (1865). Biographical information comes from Reverend George Gilfillan's 'Janet Hamilton' in her *Poems and Ballads*, pp. ix–xxxiv.

MARY HOWITT (1799–1888), poet, essayist, children's writer, translator and editor, came from a prosperous Quaker family and was partly educated at home in Uttoxeter, Staffordshire, and partly at schools organized by the Society of Friends. She developed her career as an author in conjunction with her Quaker husband, William Howitt, whom she married in 1821. Their first joint work, *The Desolation of Eyam and Other Poems* (1827), consisted of a selection of their poems and essays which they had already published in magazines. Mary Howitt taught herself Swedish and Danish, and translated Frederika Bremer's eighteen novels (1842–63) into English. For this translation work, she was awarded a silver medal from the Literary Academy of Stockholm. Although much of her writing embodies religious pieties, her poems about working-people are of interest today. Biographical information comes from *DNB* and text is reprinted from *Ballads and Other Poems*, pp. 295–7.

JEAN INGELOW (1820–97), novelist and poet, was born at Boston in Lincolnshire and moved to London in 1863. Her first work, *A Rhyming Chronicle of Incidents and Feelings* (1850), was published anonymously. Other works include *A Story of Doom and Other Poems* (1867) and three further series of *Poems* (1863, 1874 and 1885), as well as many popular novels for children and adults. She was renowned for the mock-medieval ballad, 'High Tide on the Coast of Lincolnshire'. Biographical information comes from *DNB*. The text of 'Loss and Waste' is reprinted from *Poems*, p. 137, and 'Compensation' from *Lyrical and Other Poems*, p. 131.

FRANCES ANNE (FANNY) KEMBLE (1809–93), actress, poet, memoiriste and social critic, was born into an acting family which included her father, the well-known Shakespearean actor, Charles Kemble, and her aunt, Sarah Siddons. Fanny Kemble was born in London, educated at home in Paris by her aunt, Adelaide de Camp, and spent much of her early adult life in America, where she first went on an acting tour with her father. In 1834, she married Pierce Butler, a slave-holding plantation owner in Georgia, and it was only then that she seemed to become aware of the plight of slaves in the Deep South of America. In 1847, after a shaky marriage with continual quarrelling over, *inter alia*, the issue of slavery, Butler successfully filed in Philadelphia for divorce on the grounds that she had deserted him by her extended two-year visit to England. Kemble did not, until May 1863, publish her 1838–9 memoir, *Journal of a Residence on a Georgian Plantation*, which criticized the practice of slavery in the Deep South. Slavery had been abolished in Britain by 1834, but was not outlawed in the USA until January, 1863, with Abraham Lincoln's Emancipation Proclamation. Thus her 1838–9 chronicle of injustice for black slaves on her former husband's relatively enlightened plantation ironically did not appear until just after slavery had been made illegal. Despite her liberal views which led her to write her outspoken memoir and to break the law by educating a child slave along with her daughter, Sarah, Fanny Kemble did not see slavery in the American South as a fit subject for poetry; rather, in her conventional verse, she kept to traditional themes of heterosexual love, familial love, and loss and death among Europeans. Kemble was a professional writer, in that she turned whatever she wrote into profitable books, particularly when she needed money. She and her husband disagreed over her stringent comments on Americans in her first memoir, which she sold in order to finance her dying aunt's medical and other bills. Subsequently, Kemble made most of her money by giving readings from Shakespeare in Britain, on the Continent and in the USA. Kemble's two daughters were separated from her until they reached their majority because Butler had custody of them. Her first published work was the play, *Francis I* (1827), and she later translated from the French two further plays: *An English Tragedy* (1863) and *Madame de Belle Isle* (1863). Her other works were predominantly journals and memoirs: *The Journal of a Residence in America* (1835); *A Year of Consolation* (1847); *Journal of a Residence on a Georgian Plantation 1838–1839* (1863); *Records of a Girlhood* (1878); *Records of a Later Life* (1882) and *Further Records* (1890). She wrote three collections of poetry: *Poems* (1844); *Poems* (1866); *Poems* (1883). She also wrote a farce, *The Adventures of John Timothy Homespun in Switzerland* (1889) and a novel, *Far Away and Long Ago* (1899). My biographical information comes from Dorothy Marshall, *Fanny Kemble* and J. C. Furnas, *Fanny Kemble*. Texts are taken from *Poems*, pp. 72 and 94.

MAY KENDALL (pseudonym of Emma Goldworth) (1861–?1931), poet and novelist, was also an early sociologist, assisting Seebohm Rowntree with two works of social research,

How the Labourer Lives (1913) and *The Human Needs of Labour* (1918). Her father was a Wesleyan minister, and she was born in Bridlington, Yorkshire. Her first work, *That Very Mab* (1885), was a collaborative collection of essays, stories and poems with Andrew Lang. She subsequently wrote two books of poems, *Dreams to Sell* (1887) and *Songs from Dreamland* (1894), some of which had first appeared in *Punch*, *Magazine of Art*, *St James's Magazine* and *Longman's Magazine*. Her fiction included *From a Garret* (1887), *Such is Life* (1889), *White Poppies* (1893) and *Turkish Bonds* (1898). Text is taken from *Songs from Dreamland* (1894), pp. 6–7, and biographical information comes from *The Feminist Companion to Literature in English*.

AMY LEVY (1861–89), journalist, novelist and poet, contributed many literary articles, poems and short stories to magazines such as *London Society*, *Temple Bar*, *Woman's World*, *Cambridge Review*, *Jewish Chronicle* and the *Gentleman's Magazine*. Some of these pieces were unsigned. She was born in Clapham, South London, the second daughter of Isabelle (née Levin) and Lewis Levy, a journalist. She went to school in Brighton, where her parents moved in 1876. She was the first Jewish student at Newnham College, Cambridge, and was fluent in French and German. But, according to her biographer, she suffered from an irredeemable 'melancholy' and committed suicide at her parents' home in Euston, London, one week after she had corrected the proofs of her final collection of poetry, *A London Plane-Tree and Other Verse* (1889). A 'woman poet of the first rank', Levy had concluded in relation to Christina Rossetti, 'is among those things which the world has yet to produce', (Edward Wagenknecht, 'Amy Levy' in *Daughters of the Covenant* (1983), Amherst: University of Massachusetts Press, pp. 59 and 70). Levy is here hypercritical of her own prospects as a poet, let alone the works of Elizabeth Barrett Browning, Aphra Behn or Sappho. Levy published three novels: *The Romance of a Shop* (1888); *Reuben Sachs: A Sketch* (1888, reprinted 1972); *Miss Meredith* (1889), as well as three collections of poems: *Xantippe and Other Verse* (1881); *A Minor Poet and Other Verse* (1884); and *A London Plane-Tree and Other Verse* (1889). The texts are reprinted from *A Minor Poet and Other Verse*, pp. 13–22 and *A London Plane-Tree and Other Verse*, pp. 21, 37, 51 and 53.

ALICE MEYNELL (1847–1922), poet, journalist, and essayist, was the second daughter of Thomas Thompson, the illegitimate son of Mary Edwards, a Creole of mixed English and Jamaican parentage. Alice Meynell refers to her Creole background in a poem dedicated to her daughter, 'To Olivia, of Her Dark Eyes'. Her father, who had been educated privately and later at Trinity College, Cambridge, inherited the wealth accrued from his grandfather who had owned a sugar plantation in Jamaica as well as property in Lancashire, Liverpool, and Wharf. He married Christiana Weller, a friend of Charles Dickens, and the couple led an itinerant life in Italy and England, living off the Thompson inherited wealth. Alice Meynell had a close relationship with her father who educated her and her sister, Elizabeth. Elizabeth Thompson (later Butler) became an esteemed pictorial artist who was famous for her paintings of war scenes. Alice Meynell's poetry seems to have first been fostered by a Roman Catholic priest, Father Dignam, whom she was eventually forbidden to meet because of her threat to his vow of celibacy. Alice Meynell met Father Dignam when she entered the Roman Catholic Church of her own volition in 1868. In 1875, *Preludes*, her first collection of poems, which was illustrated by her sister, appeared. She married Wilfred Meynell, a Roman Catholic and a journalist, in 1877, and both she and her husband worked in journalism to make money to support themselves and eventually their eight children, one of whom died in infancy. Alice Meynell contributed to the *Spectator*, the *Saturday Review* and the *Scots Observer* (later the *National Observer*). She befriended the poet, Francis Thompson, knew Tennyson and Ruskin, and became intimate with George Meredith and Coventry Patmore. She was a supporter of women's rights, arguing especially for equal treatment with men in the spheres of work, education and social life. A selection of her essays was published in *The Rhythm of Life* (1893), and her history of a religious order, *The Poor Sisters of Nazareth*, appeared in 1899. Biographical information comes from Viola Meynell, *Alice Meynell: A Memoir* and June Badeni, *The Slender Tree*. Texts are reprinted from *Preludes*, pp. 51–4 and 71.

CONSTANCE NADEN (1858–89), poet and philosopher, died before she could fully explore her philosophy of mind, but some of her essays were published in scientific journals during her lifetime and collected posthumously (*Induction and Deduction*, 1890). She was born in Birmingham, and when her mother died shortly after her birth, her father asked her maternal grand-parents, who were Evangelicals in the Church of England, to bring her up. From the age of eight she attended a private day school in Birmingham until she was sixteen. She became profi-cient at French, German, Latin and the elements of Greek, and she travelled with friends in Europe. She studied botany at undergraduate level from 1879 to 1881, and then enrolled as a part-time student of Physical and Biological Sciences at Mason College, Birmingham University (1881–87). She did not aim to take a degree, but, through her studies in the natural sciences, hoped to further her studies in philosophy. When she inherited money from her grandmother in 1887, she went on tour with a friend to India. Here she contracted some type of tropical fever which, after her return to London in 1888, caused her sudden death. Biographical information comes from William R. Hughes, *Constance Naden: A Memoir*, and texts are taken from *Songs and Sonnets of Springtime*, pp. 88–90, and *A Modern Apostle*, pp. 139–43.

EDITH NESBIT (1858–1924), poet and novelist for children and adults, attended two boarding-schools, which she abhorred, after the early death of her father, John Collis Nesbit, who had run the family's agricultural college. She was brought up by her widowed mother, Sarah Green Nesbit. Edith Nesbit married Hubert Bland, a clerk, who later became a freelance journalist. At first after she married, Nesbit had to earn their living by writing, while she fostered her husband's writing by her collab-oration with him in prose writing. Nesbit was pregnant by Hubert Bland before she married him, and subsequently had two more children by him. He also fathered, and Edith adopted, two children by her companion and friend, Alice Hoatson. Bland had also had a child by his mother's companion, Maggie Doran, before he married. Edith eventually reacted to Hubert's incessant philandering by having affairs herself with younger men. She is best known for her children's fiction, but she regarded herself primarily as a poet, publishing her first volume,

Lays and Legends, in 1886. George Bernard Shaw wrote in a friendly mock review of this work, 'The author has a fair ear, writes with remarkable facility and with some grace, and occasionally betrays an incisive, but shrewish insight' (quoted in Julia Briggs, *A Woman of Passion: The Life of E. Nesbit, 1858–1924*). This first collection was reprinted as *Lays and Legends*, 'First Series', accompanied by her 'Second Series' of the same title in 1892. A third collection, *Leaves of Life* (1888), was followed by *A Pomander of Verse* in 1895 and *Songs of Love and Empire* in 1898. Among her prolific potboiling stories, novels and verses for adults and children, which she wrote in her own name or under pseudonyms, are her classic children's novels which are still read today and occasionally adapted into television plays. Biographical information comes from Julia Briggs, *A Woman of Passion* and texts are reprinted from *Lays and Legends*, pp. 82–3, 91–2, 97, 150, 187 and 189, and *A Pomander of Verse*, pp. 70–1. 'Vies Manquées', her first published poem, first appeared in *Good Words* (December, 1876) with the title 'A Year Ago' (Briggs, p. 35).

CAROLINE NORTON (1808–77) (née Sheridan) was born into the Sheridan family of playwrights and actors and had *The Dandies' Rout*, a parody, published when she was eleven. She began her career as a professional poet, novelist, editor and pamphleteer after she had discovered that her marriage in 1827 with George Norton, a barrister, was not as financially stable as he had originally promised that it would be. He also abused her verbally and physically, and finally deserted her in 1836, taking their three young boys with him. He refused to allow her to have custody of them, and later that year had her close friend, Lord Melbourne, tried for 'criminal conversation', that is, adultery with her. Despite or because of Norton's solicitors' suborning of some of the Nortons' former servants, Lord Melbourne was acquitted. A few months after Lord Melbourne's trial, Caroline Norton set up house in Westminster, London, on her own, continuing to pursue the profession of author in order to keep herself. The novelist, George Meredith, modelled his eponymous heroine in *Diana of the Crossways* on her life and circumstances. Through her writing of various pamphlets, which owe their origin to her legal battles with George Norton in the divorce courts, Caroline Norton helped to reform the divorce laws so that husbands could no longer have an automatic right to custody of children or to money earned or inherited by their wives. In the last months of her life, she married Sir William Stirling-Maxwell, an old friend. Caroline Norton wrote five works of prose fiction: *The Wife, and Woman's Reward* (1835); *Stuart of Dunleath* (1851); *Lost and Saved* (1863); and *Old Sir Douglas* (1866). In addition, she edited various anthologies, and for the *Fisher's Drawing-Room Scrap-book* (1846–9), contributed all the poems. She also wrote the following collections of poetry: *The Sorrows of Rosalie, A Tale with Other Poems* (1829); *The Undying One and Other Poems* (1830); *A Voice from the Factories* (1836); *The Dream and Other Poems* (1840); *The Child of the Islands* (1845); *Aunt Carry's Ballads for Children* (1847); *Bingen on the Rhine* (undated), and *The Lady of La Garaye* (1862). Some of her pamphlets about women's rights to custody of their children were circulated privately, but two of her published pamphlets, *A Letter to the Queen on Lord Chancellor Cranworth's Marriage and Divorce Bill* (1855), and *A Review of the Divorce Bill* (1856), were very influential in modifying clauses of the Divorce Bill of 1856. Biographical information comes from Alice Acland's *Caroline Norton* and Alan Chedzoy's *A Scandalous Woman*. Texts are taken from *The Undying One and Other Poems*, pp. 178–9 and 207–8, and *The Dream and Other Poems*, pp. 286–7.

DOROTHEA MARIA OGILVY (1823–95), poet, although descended from an Earl, was interested in writing about the poor. Her books of poems include *Willie Webster's Wooing and Wedding on the Braes of Angus* (1868); *My Thoughts: Poems* (1870), and *Poems* (1873). Biographical information comes from *An Anthology of Scottish Women Poets*, pp. 356–7. Text is taken from *Poems*, pp. 112–13, but I am indebted to Catherine Kerrigan's *Anthology* for drawing my attention to this poet.

MOIRA O'NEILL (pseudonym of Agnes Nesta Shakespeare Skrine, née Higginson) (1864–1955), poet, was born in Antrim, Ireland, and married Walter Clarmont Skrine, a Protestant landowner. She wrote two books of poetry: *An Easter Vacation* (1893) and *Songs of the Glens of Antrim* (1900). Biographical information comes from *A Biographical Dictionary of Irish*

Writers. Texts are reprinted from *Songs of the Glens of Antrim*, pp. 10–11 and 49–50.

ADELAIDE ANN PROCTER (1825–64), poet, was born and brought up in London. She was educated at home in languages, art, music and mathematics. She first published her poems under the name of Mary Berwick, because she did not want her family to know her authorship. Her father, Bryan Waller Procter, a solicitor with literary aspirations, wrote under the name of Barry Cornwall and was a friend of Charles Dickens. When Adelaide Procter began contributing poems in 1853 to *Household Words*, the journal that Dickens edited, she did not want Dickens to be influenced by his friendship with her family. Adelaide Procter was also interested in rights for women, and in 1859 she was appointed by the Council for the National Association for the Promotion of Social Science to a committee which was looking into employment for women. In 1861, she edited *Victoria Regia*, a miscellany of poetry and prose which was set up in type by women compositors. In 1862, her collection of religious poems, *A Chaplet of Verse*, was published in order to benefit a night refuge for women. She collected her poems in *Legends and Lyrics* (2 vols, 1858) and these poems had gone into the tenth edition by 1866. In 1864, she died of tuberculosis at the age of thirty-nine. Biographical information comes from *DNB* and Charles Dickens' 'Memoir' in *Legends and Lyrics*. Texts are reprinted from *Legends and Lyrics*, pp. 34–6 and 155–6.

DOLLIE RADFORD (1858–1920) (née Maitland), poet, essayist and children's writer, was born in Worcester and was educated at Malvern and Queen's College, London. In 1883, she married Ernest Radford and lived in Hampstead, London. She was a socialist and a member of the Fabian Society. Her works included: *A Light Load* (1891); *Good Night* (1895); *Songs and Other Verses* (1895); and *One Way of Love: An Idyll* (1898). Text is reprinted from *Songs and Other Verses* (1895), pp. 87–91.

AGNES MARY ROBINSON (1857–1944), poet, was born in Leamington, England, but lived much of her adult life in France with her first husband, James Darmesteter, who became a professor of Zend at Paris. When he died in 1894, she married M.

Duclaux. She wrote *Songs, Ballads, and A Garden Play* (1888) and *Retrospect and Other Poems* (1893), as well as a novel and literary biographies. James Darmesteter translated some of her poems into French. Biographical information comes from *Chambers Biographical Dictionary*. Texts are taken from *Songs, Ballads and A Garden Play*, pp. 40–1, and *Retrospect and Other Poems*, p. 34.

CHRISTINA ROSSETTI (1830–94) was born into a creative family, and her reputation as a poet has been overshadowed by that of her poet-painter brother, Dante Gabriel Rossetti. Christina Rossetti was descended from Italians on both sides of her family. Her father, Gabriele Rossetti, was an exiled political radical who was born in Naples, coming to settle in London in 1824. Her mother, Frances Polidori, had an Italian-born father, Gaetano Polidori, and an English mother, Anna Maria Pearce. Frances Polidori was committed to Anglo-Catholicism, a faith to which Christina subscribed throughout her life of self-mortification. Gaetano Polidori, a teacher of Italian, was a literary man and in 1847 he published Christina's first poems on his own printing-press. Subsequently, Christina Rossetti became a writer, after a brief and unsuccessful attempt at teaching. Her contributions to the *Germ*, the short-lived periodical of the Pre-Raphaelite Brotherhood, which made the journal more significant than it otherwise would have been, tend to be overlooked in discussions about that movement. The PRB, despite the fact that it was an all-male coterie of seven, including her brothers, William Michael and Dante Gabriel, published seven of Christina's poems: 'Dreamland', 'An End', 'A Pause of Thought', 'Roses for the Flush of Youth', 'A Testimony', 'Repining' and 'Sweet Death'. Critics have sought to make biographical readings of many of Christina Rossetti's poems, particularly *Donna Innominata*, drawing on the information that she was emotionally involved with James Collinson (a member, if a dormant one, of the Pre-Raphaelite Brotherhood), Charles Bagot Cayley and, putatively, William Bell Scott. Rossetti herself implies in her epigraph that her sonnet sequence is not in her own voice, but is a fabrication of the points of view of unnamed ladies of innumerable Italian sonneteers. Dorothy Margaret Stuart points out that the 'broken betrothal motif' emerged in Rossetti's poetry before she met Collinson or Cayley

(*Christina Rossetti*, 1930, p. 17). Christina Rossetti's works include the following collections of poetry: *Verses* (1847); *Goblin Market* (1862); *The Prince's Progress and Other Poems* (1866); *A Pageant and Other Poems* (1881); *Poems* (1890). She also wrote fiction and religious prose: *Commonplace and Other Short Stories* (1870); *Annus Domini* (1874); *Speaking Likenesses* (1874); *Seek and Find* (1879), and *Maude* (published posthumously in 1897). Her other works—*Called to be Saints* (1881), *Time Flies* (1885) and *The Face of the Deep* (1892)—mixed the genres of prose and poetry. Biographical information comes from Lona Mosk Packer, *Christina Rossetti*. The texts of 'When I am Dead . . .', 'Oh Roses for the Flush of Youth', 'Remember', 'The Bourne', 'A Triad', 'A Birthday', 'Winter: My Secret', 'Goblin Market', 'The Queen of Hearts' and 'A Christmas Carol' come from *The Complete Poems of Christina Rossetti*, pp. 11–26, 29, 36–7, 40, 47, 58, 132–3, 142 and 216–7; the texts of the sonnets from *Donna Innominata* are reprinted from *Christina Rossetti, The Poetical Works*, pp. 50–9.

DORA SIGERSON (1866–1918), poet, one of two daughters of Dr George Sigerson, a professor of zoology and a poet, and Hester Varian, poet and novelist, was born and brought up in Dublin as a Roman Catholic and took up her family's Republican sympathies. In 1896, she emigrated to London when she married Clement Shorter, editor of the *Illustrated London News*. Her volumes of verse include *Verse* (1893); *The Fairy Changeling and Other Poems* (1897); *My Lady's Slipper and Other Poems* (1898) and *Ballards and Poems* (1899). Biographical information comes from *The Poets of Ireland*, and texts are reprinted from *The Fairy Changeling and Other Poems*, pp. 70–1, 77, and *Ballads and Poems*, pp. 87–8.

MARGARET VELEY (1843–87), poet, was the second of four daughters of Augustus Charles Veley, a solicitor in Braintree, Essex. Her mother was the daughter of a country rector. Although she spent one term at a boarding-school, Queen's College, in London, she was mainly educated at home by governesses and masters. Margaret Veley began writing poetry at the age of fourteen, and during her relatively short lifetime, had a few poems published in the *Spectator*, *Blackwood's*

Magazine, and the *Cornhill Magazine*. When her father died in 1878, Margaret Veley moved to London with her mother. Here the poet gained entrance to literary circles, catching the attention of Leslie Stephen, who edited and introduced her sole book of poems, *A Marriage of Shadows and Other Poems*, which was published posthumously in 1888. Biographical information comes from Leslie Stephen's preface to that work, and texts are from pp. 115–6 and 123.

AUGUSTA WEBSTER (née Davies) (1837–94), poet, dramatist and translator, was the grand-daughter of Joseph Hume, friend of Hazlitt, Lamb and Godwin. Her father was a Vice-Admiral, and Augusta was educated at a school in Banff, Scotland, and then at the Cambridge School of Art. She also taught herself Greek, French, Italian and Spanish. In 1863, she married Thomas Webster, a lawyer, and had one child, a daughter. Prior to marriage, she had already written a book of poems, *Blanche Lisle, and Other Poems* (1860), which was published under the pseudonym of Cecil Home. In 1864, she wrote a novel, *Lesley's Guardians*, and a poem, *Lilian Gray*, both of which appeared under her pseudonym. But her Greek translations and subsequent volumes of verse appeared under her own name. Her collections of poetry include: *Dramatic Studies* (1866); *A Woman Sold and Other Poems* (1867); *Portraits* (1870); *A Book of Rhyme* (1881), and an uncompleted sonnet sequence *Mother and Daughter* which was published posthumously in 1895. She also translated verse dramas from the Greek, as well as composing verse dramas, only one of which, *In a Day*, was performed on stage. She actively supported women's suffrage and better education for women, and in 1878 a volume of her essays, *A Housewife's Opinions*, was reprinted from the *Examiner*. Biographical information comes from *DNB*, and texts are taken from *Mother and Daughter: An Uncompleted Sonnet Sequence*, pp. 30, 38, 39 and 41.

MARGARET LOUISA WOODS (née Bradley) (1856–1945), novelist and poet, was born at Rugby, daughter of the Dean of Westminster. In 1879, she married the Reverend Henry George Woods, who was president of Trinity College, Oxford between

1887 and 1897. She wrote a novel, *A Village Tragedy* (1887), as well as *Lyrics and Ballads* (1889) and *Aeromancy and Other Poems* (1896). Biographical information comes from *Chambers Biographical Dictionary* and the text comes from *Lyrics and Ballads*, pp. 14–16.

NOTE ON THE EDITOR

JENNIFER BREEN, Senior Lecturer at the School of Literary and Media Studies, University of North London, has lectured in Britain and abroad on Romantic poetry, Victorian poetry, and twentieth-century literature. Dr Breen has edited *Wilfred Owen: Selected Poetry and Prose* (1988) and *Women Romantic Poets, 1785–1832: An Anthology*, and is author of *In Her Own Write: Twentieth-Century Women's Fiction* (1990).

CHRONOLOGY OF EVENTS: 1830–1901

Year	Literary & Artistic Events	Historical Events
1830	Caroline Norton, *The Undying One* Alfred Tennyson, *Poems, Chiefly Lyrical* William Cobbett, *Rural Rides*	Railways begin
1832		Reform Bill
1833	Robert Browning, *Pauline* Alfred Tennyson, *Poems* Newman *et al*, *Tracts for the Times* (1833–41)	
1834		Abolition of slavery in British Empire
1835	Robert Browning, *Paracelsus* Eliza Cook, *Lays of a Wild Harp* Fanny Kemble, *Journal of a Residence in America* Sara Coleridge, *Phantasmion*	
1836	Caroline Norton, *A Voice from the Factories*	
1837		Accession of Queen Victoria University of London Incorporated
1838	Eliza Cook, *Melaia and Other Poems*	Anti-Corn Law League Chartism begins
1839	Margaret Carpenter, *The Sisters* (oil painting)	Chartist Riots
1840	Caroline Norton, *The Dream and Other Poems* Robert Browning, *Sordello*	Penny Post Queen's marriage to Prince Albert
1841		Peel PM New Zealand declared British

Year	Literary & Artistic Events	Historical Events
1842	Female Schools of Art founded by the government	Chartist Riots Income Tax Mines Act Copyright Act
1843	Macaulay, *Critical & Historical Essays*	Natal British
1844	Elizabeth Barrett, *Poems* Fanny Kemble, *Poems* Coventry Patmore, *Poems*	Factory Act Co-op Movement
1845	Eliza Cook, *Poems*, 2nd Series Caroline Norton, *The Child of the Islands*	Newman converts to Catholicism Irish famine
1846	Currer, Ellis and Acton Bell (Brontës), *Poems*	Russell PM Repeal of Corn Laws
1847	Anne Brontë, *Agnes Grey* Charlotte Brontë, *Jane Eyre* Emily Brontë, *Wuthering Heights* Christina Rossetti, *Verses* Alfred Tennyson, *The Princess*	Ten Hours Factory Act Foundation of Communist League
1848	Anne Brontë, *The Tenant of Wildfell Hall* Dora Greenwell, *Poems* Elizabeth Gaskell, *Mary Barton*	Communist Manifesto Queen's College School founded
1849	Charlotte Brontë, *Shirley* *Eliza Cook's Journal* *Household Words*, ed. Charles Dickens Macaulay, *History of England*	
1850	Pre-Raphaelite Brotherhood, *The Germ* Robert Browning, *Christmas Eve & Easter Day* Elizabeth Barrett Browning, *Sonnets from the Portuguese* Alfred Tennyson, *In Memoriam*	Public Libraries Act North London Collegiate School founded
1851		Goldrush in Australia Great Exhibition
1852	Matthew Arnold, *Empedocles on Etna & Other Poems* Harriet Beecher Stowe, *Uncle Tom's Cabin*	Derby and Aberdeen PMs

Year	Literary & Artistic Events	Historical Events
1853	Matthew Arnold, *Poems* Charlotte Brontë, *Villette* Elizabeth Gaskell, *Ruth*	
1854	Alfred Tennyson, *The Charge of the Light Brigade*	Crimean War Working Men's College
1855	Matthew Arnold, *Poems*, 2nd Series Robert Browning, *Men and Women* Elizabeth Gaskell, *North and South* Caroline Norton, *A Letter to the Queen* Rosa Bonheur *The Horse Fair* (oil painting)	Palmerston PM Florence Nightingale in Crimea
1856	Elizabeth Barrett Browning, *Aurora Leigh* Caroline Norton, *A Review of the Divorce Bill* Coventry Patmore, *Espousals*	Crimean War ends School for Nurses at St Thomas's Hospital
1857	Charlotte Brontë, *The Professor* *Englishwoman's Review* founded Society of Female Artists founded	Indian Mutiny Matrimonial Causes Act
1858	George Eliot, *Scenes from Clerical Life* Adelaide A. Procter, *Legends and Lyrics* Emma Brownlow, *The Foundling Restored to its Mother* (oil painting) *Englishwoman's Journal* founded	Derby PM
1859	George Eliot, *Adam Bede* J. S. Mill, *On Liberty* Charles Darwin, *The Origin of Species*	Palmerston PM Franco–Austrian War

Year	Literary & Artistic Events	Historical Events
1860	George Eliot, *The Mill on the Floss* Coventry Patmore, *Faithful For Ever* Augusta Webster, *Blanche Lisle and Other Poems*	Lincoln US President Italian Unity Food and Drugs Act Society for Employment of Women
1861	George Eliot, *Silas Marner* J. S. Mill, *Representative Government* Emily Mary Osborn, *The Escape of Lord Nithsdale* (oil painting)	American Civil War Death of Prince Albert
1862	George Meredith, *Modern Love* Christina Rossetti, *Goblin Market*	
1863	Elizabeth Gaskell, *Sylvia's Lovers* George Eliot, *Romola* Janet Hamilton, *Poems & Essays* Jean Ingelow, *Poems*, 1st Series Fanny Kemble, *Journal of a Georgian Residence* J. S. Mill, *Utilitarianism* Emma Brownlow, *The Christening* (oil painting)	
1864	Robert Browning, *Dramatis Personae* Eliza Cook, *New Echoes & Other Poems* Alfred Tennyson, *Enoch Arden* Augusta Webster, *Lilian Gray*	Female Medical Society established
1865	Matthew Arnold, *Essays in Criticism* Lewis Carroll, *Alice in Wonderland* *Pall Mall Gazette*	Russell PM Abraham Lincoln assassinated American Civil War ends Women's Suffrage Movement established

Year	Literary & Artistic Events	Historical Events
1866	George Eliot, *Felix Holt* Elizabeth Gaskell, *Wives & Daughters* Fanny Kemble, *Poems* Christina Rossetti, *The Prince's Pageant & Other Poems* A. C. Swinburne, *Poems & Ballads*, 1st Series Augusta Webster, *Dramatic Studies*	Derby PM Riots in Ireland Mendel's laws of heredity War between Austria, Prussia and Italy
1867	Mathilde Blind, *Poems* Augusta Webster, *A Woman Sold & Other Poems* Karl Marx, *Das Kapital*, Vol. I	Disraeli PM Second Reform Bill Canadian Independence Matrimonial Causes Act
1868	Robert Browning, *The Ring and the Book* Janet Hamilton, *Poems & Ballads*	Gladstone PM
1869	Matthew Arnold, *Culture & Anarchy* J. S. Mill, *On the Subjection of Women*	Suez Canal Cambridge University admits women to lectures
1870	Dante Gabriel Rossetti, *Poems* Augusta Webster, *Portraits*	Franco–Prussian War Elementary Education Act
1871	Lewis Carroll, *Through the Looking-Glass* George Eliot, *Middlemarch* Charles Darwin, *Descent of Man* Walt Whitman, *Passage to India*	Trade unions now legal
1872	Charles Darwin, *Expression of the Emotions in Man and Animals* Thomas Hardy, *Under the Greenwood Tree*	Secret Ballot
1873	Thomas Hardy, *A Pair of Blue Eyes* Henrietta Ward, *Chatterton* (oil painting)	Typewriters

Year	Literary & Artistic Events	Historical Events
1874	George Eliot, *The Legend of Jubal and Other Poems* Elizabeth Thompson Butler, *Calling the Roll after an Engagement, Crimea* (oil painting)	Disraeli PM
1875	Katharine Bradley, *The New Minnesinger*	
1876	George Eliot, *Daniel Deronda* Jean Ingelow, *Poems*, 2nd Series Alice Meynell, *Preludes*	Dr Elizabeth Garrett, first woman doctor
1877	Coventry Patmore, *The Unknown Eros and Other Poems* Evelyn Pickering de Morgan, *Aurora Triumphans* (oil painting)	Russo–Turkish War Annexation of the Transvaal
1878	A. C. Swinburne, *Poems & Ballads*, 2nd Series Augusta Webster, *A Housewife's Opinions* Charles Groves, *Dictionary of Music* (finished 1899)	Congress of Berlin Oxford University admits women to lectures London University degrees for women
1879	George Eliot, *Impressions of Theophrastus*	
1880	Alfred Tennyson, *Ballads & Other Poems*	Gladstone PM Free compulsory primary education Transvaal becomes a republic
1881	Michael Field, *Bellerophon & Other Poems* Amy Levy, *Xantippe & Other Verse* Constance Naden, *Songs & Sonnets of Springtime* Christina Rossetti, *The Pageant & Other Poems* Dante Gabriel Rossetti, *Ballads & Sonnets* Augusta Webster, *A Book of Rhyme* Oscar Wilde, *Poems*	Married Women's Property Act Irish Land Act

Year	Literary & Artistic Events	Historical Events
1882	Fanny Kemble, *Poems*	
1883	Olive Schreiner, *Story of an African Farm*	
1884	Amy Levy, *A Minor Poet and Other Verse*	Third Reform Bill Oxford English Dictionary Fabian Society founded
1885	Alfred Tennyson, *Tiresias & Other Poems* George Meredith, *Diana of the Crossways* Jean Ingelow, *Poems*, 3rd Series Karl Marx, *Das Kapital*, Vol. II *Dictionary of National Biography*, Vol. I	Salisbury PM European division of Africa
1886	George Eliot, *The Spanish Gypsy* Thomas Hardy, *The Mayor of Casterbridge* Edith Nesbit, *Lays & Legends*	Gladstone and Salisbury PMs
1887	Constance Naden, *A Modern Apostle*	Queen's Golden Jubilee Rational Dress Society founded
1888	Edith Nesbit, *Leaves of Life* Agnes Mary F. Robinson, *Songs, Ballads & A Garden Play* Margaret Veley, *A Marriage of Shadows & Other Poems* Margaret L. Woods, *Lyrics*	County Councils begin
1889	Michael Field, *Long Ago* A. C. Swinburne, *Poems & Ballads*, 3rd Series Alfred Tennyson, *Demeter & Other Poems* Margaret L. Woods, *Lyrics & Ballads* W. B. Yeats, *Wanderings of Oisin*	London dock strike
1890	Christina Rossetti, *Poems* Emily Dickenson, *Poems*, 1st Series William Morris founds the Kelmscott Press William James, *Principles of Psychology*	

Year	Literary & Artistic Events	Historical Events
1891	Emily Dickinson, *Poems*, 2nd Series *Faber Book of Modern Verse*, ed. Michael Roberts	Free elementary education
1892	Michael Field, *Sight & Song* Edith Nesbit, *Lays & Legends*, 2nd Series Alfred Tennyson, *Death of Oenone & Other Poems*	Gladstone PM
1893	Mathilde Blind, *Songs & Sonnets* Michael Field, *Underneath the Bough*	Labour Representation Committee (precursor of Labour Party starts)
1894	Agnes Mary F. Robinson, *Retrospect and Other Poems* *The Yellow Book* Sidney and Beatrice Webb, *History of Trade Unionism*	Rosebery PM
1895	Edith Nesbit, *A Pomander of Verse* Dollie Radford, *Songs & Other Verses* Augusta Webster, *Mother & Daughter* W. B. Yeats, *Poems* Karl Marx, *Das Kapital*, Vol. III	Salisbury PM
1896	Mary E. Coleridge, *Fancy's Following* Margaret L. Woods, *Aeromancy & Other Poems* A. E. Housman, *A Shropshire Lad* Emily Dickenson, *Poems*, 3rd Series *Savoy*, ed. Arthur Symons	
1897	Mary E. Coleridge, *Fancy's Guerdon* Christina Rossetti, *Maude* Mary Kingsley, *Travels in West Africa* Sidney & Beatrice Webb, *Industrial Democracy*	Queen Victoria's Diamond Jubilee Klondike goldrush

Year	Literary & Artistic Events	Historical Events
1898	Edith Nesbit, *Songs of Love & Empire* Dora Sigerson, *The Fairy Changeling & Other Poems*	
1899	Amy Levy, *A London Plane-Tree & Other Verse* Dora Sigerson, *Ballads & Poems* W. B. Yeats, *The Wind Among the Reeds*	War in South Africa Board of Education
1900	Moira O'Neill, *Songs of the Glens of Antrim* Sigmund Freud, *The Interpretation of Dreams* British Library catalogue (books to 1880) *Oxford Book of English Verse*, ed. Arthur Quiller-Couch	Relief of Mafeking
1901	Thomas Hardy, *Poems of Past and Present* W. B. Yeats, *Poems* Sigmund Freud, *The Psychopathology of Everyday Life*	Queen Victoria dies Federation of Australia

INTRODUCTION

From 1830 to 1900 in Victorian Britain the publication of creative writing by women increased substantially, along with the increase in the publication of printed matter generally. On the one hand, the numbers who became literate grew steadily, especially after the Education Act of 1870. On the other, with the introduction of the Fourdrinier papermaking machines in 1807, steam printing in 1814 and more efficient book distribution after 1830 via the new railways and steamships, the publishing industry expanded rapidly to meet rising demand, so that many more authors could make their living by writing for publication.[1] The contribution of women authors to this growth in publishing is now more easily explored because of the recent appearance of various dictionaries and checklists of women's creative writing. According to R. C. Alston, in his Introduction to *A Checklist of Women Writers, 1801–1900*, from approximately one hundred works in 1830, literature by women reached its peak in 1890 with the publication of at least five hundred and fifty works of poetry, drama or fiction by women in that year. And, as Alston notes, these figures are not 'comprehensive'.[2]

The novels of a few Victorian women authors, such as George Eliot, the Brontë sisters and Elizabeth Gaskell have been available since their first publication. Yet, though it is now possible to discover the titles of many of the neglected works of fiction, drama and poetry which women wrote during the Victorian age, even the most interesting of these neglected works are not generally available. This is the first representative anthology of Victorian women's poetry. Thirty-one women poets who published their work between 1830 and 1900 are included here.

Some readers might regard Felicia Hemans (1793–1835) and Letitia Elizabeth Landon (1802–38) as early Victorian poets, but their poetry was almost entirely written and published in the Romantic period and a selection from their poetry is included in my earlier *Women Romantic Poets, 1785–1832: An Anthology* (1992). Also, although Joanna Baillie (1762–1851) lived long after Queen Victoria acceded to the throne, most of Baillie's lyric poetry was first published in 1790 and is as indicative of Romantic themes as Burns' or Wordsworth's poetry is. Dorothy Wordsworth (1771–1855) saw even more of the Victorian period than did Joanna Baillie, but, because of her subject matter and forms, her poetry is of the Romantic period. The same considerations apply to other women poets whom I have included in *Women Romantic Poets, 1785–1832*: Matilda Bethem (1776–1852), Anne Grant (1755–1853), Mary Lamb (1764–1847), Carolina Nairne (1766–1845) and Amelia Opie (1769–1853). Although Emily Brontë (1818–48) is sometimes included in Romantic anthologies, a selection of her poems along with her sisters' poetry was first published in 1846, which is well into the Victorian era. And even though Elizabeth Barrett published two books of poetry as early as 1829, the bulk of her work, both chronologically and thematically, can be placed firmly in the Victorian period.

SOCIAL, EDUCATIONAL AND LITERARY CONTEXT OF VICTORIAN WOMEN'S AUTHORSHIP

The Victorian reading public increasingly read prose in preference to poetry. Many significant novels by women authors such as the Brontës and George Eliot were acclaimed by Victorian critics and readers. Among the few women poets' works that received a comparable reception were Christina Rossetti's *Goblin Market* (1862) and Elizabeth Barrett Browning's novel in blank verse, *Aurora Leigh* (1856), which went through thirteen editions by 1873.

Alfred Lord Tennyson (1809–92) and Robert Browning (1812–89) attracted most attention from critics and readers of contemporary poetry, although other male poets such as Arthur Hugh Clough (1819–61), George Meredith (1828–1909), Matthew Arnold (1822–88), A. G. Swinburne (1837–1909), D. G. Rossetti (1828–82), Coventry Patmore (1823–96), and William Morris (1834–96) also received praise from critics as well as finding readers among the general public. For their inspiration, these poets tended either to revert to traditional religious icons and legends for literary symbols or to conjure up a non-religious spirituality or to invent a passion-and-art emotionalism in order to create a poetic mythology which might stand up to Victorian scientific and material progress. Tennyson in his elegy, *In Memoriam* (1850), engaged with many of the scientific, social and cultural issues of his day. And Browning's dramatic monologues, such as *My Last Duchess* (1842), showed at their best a percipient understanding of human psychology, as did Meredith's sonnet sequence, *Modern Love* (1892). The most interesting Victorian women poets engage with many of these same themes, but comparisons between, for example, Barrett Browning's love sonnets and Meredith's, or Christina Rossetti's *Goblin Market* and Browning's psychological monologues, or Constance Naden's social satires and Matthew Arnold's social commentary poems, reveal interesting divergences in outlook, style, imagery and tone.

Poetry generally in the Victorian period, despite the deference towards Shelley's large claims in his *Defence of Poetry* (1821; pub. 1840), slowly diminished in social importance in the face of the spirit of scientific enquiry and technical application that increasingly came to dominate in both material and spiritual life. Among the many scientific and technological developments, scientific theories of evolution which were based on earlier paleontological and biological evidence emerged in the works of Herbert Spencer (1820–1903), Alfred Wallace (1823–1913) and Charles Darwin (1809–92). New observations in astronomy together with the biological postulate that mankind had evolved in a chain from earlier species led rightly or wrongly to major revisions in assumptions about the origins of life and of the universe; this in turn influenced much of the Victorian enquiry into the reasons for the status quo of social institutions and Christian belief. Responses to theories about evolution were complex and contradictory; for example, some polemicists drew the parallel that human relations are and should be ruled by the biological doctrine of 'survival of the fittest', whereas other Victorian polemicists thought that evolutionary theory in conjunction with Benthamite utilitarianism supported an ideal of social progress based on improvement in or even the perfectibility of human nature.

J. S. Mill (1806–73), one of the most respected exponents of the possibility of human improvement, included women in his philosophical exploration of possibilities for the enhancement of human life, 'every step in improvement [for mankind] has been so invariably accompanied by a step made in raising the social position of women, that historians and philosophers have been led to adopt their elevation or debasement as on the whole the surest test and most correct measure of the civilization of a people or an age' (*The Subjection of Women*, 1869).[3] Despite Mills' publication of this progressive political philosophy about the desirability of reform of social and political institutions in relation to women, the changes he and Mary Wollstonecraft (1759–97) had advocated took place only gradually. In fact, women's achievement of a 'civil existence'[4] in British law did not begin in any significant way until the passing of the Married Women's Property Acts of 1870–82. Even the limited enfranchisement of women over thirty, following the much-delayed enfranchisement of all men, did not take place until 1918.[5]

Improvements in women's education, however, and the possibility of their consequent entrance into men's trades and professions, accelerated gradually from 1830 onwards. Independent schools for girls on the same footing as those for boys began to be established to meet the demands of middle-class parents: in 1848, Queen's College School in central London was founded for the formal education of governesses, who were employed to teach middle- and upper-class children at home. This was followed by the foundation of the North London Collegiate School in 1850 and several other similar private grammar schools subsequently. Universal elementary education was increasingly advocated by such women as Augusta Webster, who had herself had the benefit of an education at a school in Banff, Scotland, and at an Arts College in Cambridge, England. The 1870 Education Act, the climax of such advocacy, provided for universal elementary education, so that all girls as well as boys had the possibility of achieving literacy. In post-secondary education, several teacher training colleges—whose trainee teachers were mostly women—were established at that time in order to staff the National Schools and subsequent Council Schools. In the field of scientific medical care, women began to set up their own nurses' training establishments such as Florence Nightingale's School for Nurses at St Thomas's Hospital, London, in 1856. Prior to this, in 1854, the London Electric Telegraph Company began to train women as clerks. In 1878 the University of London admitted female students to full degree

awards. Cambridge University admitted women to lectures in
1869 and Oxford followed suit in 1878.[6]

Progress in making further and higher education available
generally and to women in particular was slow, however, and
even by the 1920s approximately only half of one per cent (that
is, one in two hundred) of all eighteen-year-old girls—compared
to approximately thirteen times more boys—went on to higher
education.[7] The few women who sought a professional career
usually had little choice but to enter nursing, or the lower-paid
levels of the civil service or teaching. Most women in paid
employment—29 per cent of the workforce by 1911—worked
in factories, offices or domestic service.[8]

Nevertheless, the development of formal educational oppor-
tunities for girls as well as the effects of self-education among
women resulted in a steady increase in the number of potential
women readers and writers. Authorship was paid work which
literate married and single women from all classes could under-
take if they had a talent for it. Such work could be done at home
where upper- and middle-class women particularly were
expected to spend their time. A considerable number of work-
ing-class women in factories, offices, or domestic service also
took the opportunity to read books and periodicals, and several
also wrote a wide range of books and articles.[9]

Paid employment outside the home often had to be given up
when a woman married, so one of the advantages of taking up
the vocation of author was that if a single woman became a
skilled professional writer, she could continue to develop her
career after she married, as did Elizabeth Barrett Browning,
Alice Meynell and Augusta Webster. These three women pro-
duced a great deal of poetry and other writing over lengthy
careers, and were among a considerable number of women who
considered themselves to be professional authors.

In fact, the poets in this anthology are all women who
established themselves in authorship as a vocation rather than
as a sign of an accomplishment. The writing of poems in order
to demonstrate the attainment of one of the desirable accom-
plishments for women had occasionally formed a part of upper-
and middle-class social life during the eighteenth century and
continued to some extent in the nineteenth century. But during
the Victorian period an increasing number of women—
especially across the wide range of the self-improving working

classes and the middle classes—began to take up the new
opportunities to achieve some degree of equality with men.
Gradually they became more prominent in the arts, competing
with men as professional performers, as pictorial artists, and,
not least, as authors: more women set themselves up in full-time
careers as authors than had done previously, even if a few of
them, including Mathilde Blind, Augusta Webster and the
Brontë sisters, thought that their writing would be more accept-
able if it were first to appear under a male pseudonym.

Most of the middle-class women poets who are included here
published their poetry—apart from some of their juvenilia—
with profit-making publishers. In the case of Margaret Woods
and Mary Elizabeth Coleridge, however, their first books of
poetry appeared from a private printing-press—that of C. H. O.
Daniel, the Provost of Worcester College, Oxford. And Anne,
Emily, and Charlotte Brontë (under the pseudonyms of Acton,
Ellis and Currer Bell), with a legacy from their aunt, paid for
the publication of their first collection of poems in 1846.

Of the working-class poets reprinted here, Janet Hamilton
began her career late in life. Although she wrote twenty or so
poems as a young woman, she brought up her seven surviving
children before she emerged as a poet and essayist at the age of
fifty-six. Eliza Cook, who was the daughter of a tinsmith and
brazier, and self-taught, published her first book of poetry, *Lays
of A Wild Harp* (1835), when she was only seventeen. She later
founded her own magazine, *Eliza Cook's Journal* (1849–54), in
order to provide better-educated working people with a journal
that catered to their interests. She wrote much of the material in
it and later republished it as *Jottings from My Journal* (1860).[10]
Thus all the poets in this anthology could be termed 'pro-
fessional' authors, in that writing was an occupation in which
they could earn some money or a vocation to which they could
devote their lives.

THEMES AND FORMS OF VICTORIAN WOMEN'S POETRY

Although some of these Victorian women poets published their
work in periodicals which were inaugurated by male coteries
such as the 'Pre-Raphaelite Brotherhood' and the later 'Aes-
thetes', 'Decadents' and 'Symbolists', these women poets rarely
fit neatly into these categories. None of these poets could be

'pre-Raphaelite', for example, in the way that pre-Raphaelite men saw their women subjects as objects of men's idealized longings, although a few of Christina Rossetti's early poems were first published in the *Germ*, the short-lived pre-Raphaelite periodical. Katharine Bradley and Edith Cooper ('Michael Field') had interests that were common among the 'Aesthetes', in that they valued 'art for art's sake', but when 1880s 'aestheticism' transmogrified itself into 1890s' 'decadence', these two writers drew back. At first they planned to contribute to the sensational *The Yellow Book*, in which Max Beerbohm proselytized about the 'artificial' being 'natural' to society, but they withdrew their support after Aubrey Beardsley's satiric drawings caused *The Yellow Book* (1896–8) to be generally villified. The few women poets who did contribute to *The Yellow Book* included Edith Nesbit and Dollie Radford; but they presented themselves as 'New Woman' poets rather than 'Decadent' poets.

In fact, Victorian women's poetry might be more usefully discussed under the two headings of 'post-Romantic' poets and 'New Woman' poets. The 'post-Romantics' *inter alia* moved on from Romantic representations of Nature to new appraisals of the natural world in relation to urban and industrial expansions or to Victorian scientific and religious preoccupations. Various poems in this vein were written by Mathilde Blind, the Brontë sisters, Mary Elizabeth Coleridge, Eliza Cook, George Eliot, Dora Greenwell, Mary Howitt, Jean Ingelow, Frances Kemble, Alice Meynell, Caroline Norton, Christina Rossetti, Margaret Veley, and Margaret Woods. On the other hand, the 'New Woman' poets foreshadowed the realism and satire of poetry of the early twentieth-century in their variations on the theme of women's attempts to realize their full status in society. These 'New Woman' poets included Elizabeth Barrett Browning, Michael Field, May Kendall, Amy Levy, Constance Naden, Edith Nesbit, Moira O'Neill, Adelaide Anne Procter, Dollie Radford, Agnes Mary Robinson, Dora Sigerson, and Augusta Webster. Additionally, the Scottish dialect poets Dorothea May Ogilvy and Janet Hamilton can be seen to have emerged from the Romantic tradition of Joanna Baillie and Robert Burns as well as to be addressing the preoccupations of the 'New Woman'.

The 'post-Romantic' women poets of the early (1830–50) and 'high' (1850–80) Victorian period are often surprisingly modern in their interests, if not in their use of forms. Unlike their immediate predecessors in the Romantic period (1785–1832), some of these 'post-Romantics' attempted to encapsulate in their poems the feelings of alienation and isolation from the urbanization in which, by the second half of the nineteenth century, many of them lived. For example, George Eliot's poem, 'In A London Drawingroom' (1865), foreshadows twentieth-century poetry in its description of the consequences of increased commercialization and industrialization:

> The world seems one huge prison-house and court
> Where men are punished at the slightest cost,
> With lowest rate of colour, warmth and joy.

Eliot's use of blank verse catches the anomie of a London existence which the poet perceives as both anonymous and spiritually impoverishing. Margaret Veley also in her lyric, 'A Town Garden', uses the language of realism in her representation of Nature in an urban setting:

> A garden caught in a brick-built trap,
>   Where men make money, buy and sell;
> And struggling through the stagnant haze,
>   Dim flowers, with sapless leaf and stem,
> Look up with something of the gaze
>   That homesick eyes have cast on them.

Both Eliot's and Veley's poems strike a departure in imagery and content from Mary Robinson's blank-verse poem 'London's Summer Morning' (1806) in which, half a century earlier, she had positively celebrated London's street life.

In a series of eleven Shakespearian sonnets, 'Brother and Sister' (1869), George Eliot epitomizes her 'post-Romantic' situation by contrasting this new world with the country childhood she had shared with her older brother. In the second sonnet of this series, for example, she describes her earliest memories of the sweetness of that rural idyll:

> The firmaments of daisies since to me
> Have had those mornings in their opening eyes,
> The bunchèd cowslip's pale transparency
> Carries that sunshine of sweet memories.
>
> And wild-rose branches take their finest scent
> From those blest hours of infantine content.

Such imagery evokes the pre-Victorian notion of Nature as 'mother', but she concludes by referring to the pathos of her alienation from that countryside and from her brother.

Other 'post-Romantic' poets show a comparable disillusion with Romantic notions about the permanence of experiences of spiritual nurturing or of transcendence in Nature. Some of the Brontës' poems, for example, represent a desire in the first-person speaker for a return to a prelapsarian state of innocence in the natural world yet these poems conclude with a turning-away from such a Romantic faith. Alice Meynell, in 'The Poet to His Childhood' (1875), even queries Wordsworth's represen-tation of the 'child as father to the man', by implying that the choice of the vocation of poet in childhood might serve to unman the poet in old age.

Romantic passion and sexual love appealed to some of these 'post-Romantics', but, unlike their female predecessors in the Romantic period, Victorian women poets on the whole did not adopt a male persona when the theme was heterosexual love. Although English love poetry—apart from the works of a few exceptions such as the seventeenth-century Aphra Behn and the eighteenth-century Lady Mary Wortley Montagu—was more or less a masculine tradition, women poets in the Victorian era began to adapt the tradition in order to accommodate women's passionate feelings about men as well as about other women. Letitia Elizabeth Landon and Mary Robinson had begun in the Romantic Period to effect this change by using female narrators, and Christina Rossetti later extended this new mode by writing love poetry from the point of view of the heroines who had not had their own voices in an exclusively male tradition.

In her sequence of eleven love sonnets, *Donna Innominata* (pre-1882), which she expressly wrote in competition with Elizabeth Barrett Browning's *Sonnets from the Portuguese* (1847), Christina Rossetti asserts that she is constructing from a woman's point of view a female heroine who can stand com-parison with the Dante-Petrarch tradition:

These heroines [Beatrice and Laura] of world-wide fame were preceded by a bevy of unnamed ladies, 'donne innominate', sung by a school of less conspicuous poets . . . Had such a lady spoken for herself, the portrait left us might have appeared more tender, if less dignified, than any drawn even by a devoted friend. Or had the Great Poetess of our own day and nation only been unhappy

instead of happy, her circumstances would have invited her to
bequeath to us, in lieu of the 'Portuguese Sonnets', an inimitable
'donna innominata' drawn not from fancy but from feeling, and
worthy to occupy a niche beside Beatrice and Laura (Preface).[11]

In this epigraph, Rossetti implies that because *Sonnets from the
Portuguese* are in the voice of a happily beloved and fulfilled
woman poet, they are not comparable to the love poetry of
Petrarch and Dante, which is predicated on the male narrator
not attaining the beloved. In her own sequence, she attempts to
create the authentic voice of the 'beloved' or the unattainable
'unnamed lady' of Italian love poetry. It seems pointless to
speculate about whether Rossetti actually experienced such a
hopeless love or not: she is subverting a masculine tradition of
love poetry and not necessarily representing her own personal
experience of love.

Christina Rossetti is among those 'post-Romantics' who
wrote poetry about the postponement or sublimation of sexual
love as part of the traditional idealization of women's roles. Yet
in some of her poems, especially those published during the long
period of Victorian social reforms, we can detect a note of
disquiet at and discontent with women's lot: despite her rejec-
tion of women's suffrage, Rossetti appeared to anticipate the
'New Woman' who began to seek, through education and
legislation, a new role for women in relation to men in particular
and society in general. In 'A Triad' (1856), for example, Rossetti
touches on the theme of death in life for women, and Mary
Elizabeth Coleridge in 'The Other Side of the Mirror' (1896)
symbolically represents Victorian woman's repressed sexuality.

Several 'New Woman' poets, among them Edith Nesbit and
Adelaide Anne Procter, wrote realistic love lyrics about their
contemporary experiences seen from a woman's point of view
or observations of heterosexual relationships. In 'The Wife of
All Ages' (1886) Edith Nesbit encapsulates the 'slavery' of
women who are compelled by society to abide by double
standards in the unwritten rules about 'love' between men and
women. In her poem 'Love and Knowledge' (1886) the narrator
suggests ironically that romantic love is founded on *not* under-
standing the beloved person completely. Nesbit's 'Song' (1886),
however, is more optimistic in its implication that 'true love'
and friendship between men and women can be inextricably

intertwined. And Katharine Bradley and Edith Cooper—
'Michael Field'—show, in 'Across a Gaudy Room' (1893) and
'Second Thoughts' (undated), that gender is unimportant in the
representation of spiritual intimacy between two people.

In relation to the theme of actual motherhood rather than
Romantic ideas about Nature mothering men, Augusta Webster
wrote a series of autobiographical sonnets about her love for
her only child, a daughter. These sonnets, which were first
published posthumously as *Mother and Daughter* in 1895,
anticipate twentieth-century poets' representations of personal
feelings, in colloquial diction, about motherhood.

Other women poets explored different aspects of female
creativity, particularly that of authorship. Elizabeth Barrett
Browning, for example, created a feminist poet—the epitome of
New Womanhood—as the heroine of her long blank verse
novel, *Aurora Leigh* (1856). And Amy Levy, who committed
suicide in 1889, successfully fabricated in 'A Minor Poet' (1884)
the first-person voice of a male poet, who, like herself, was
driven to suicide in circumstances of neglect and isolation.

Some of these 'New Woman' poets demonstrate an urbane
wit in poems about women's attempts to be free and equal
human beings in the face of men's efforts to keep them in a
subservient position. Constance Naden, for example, who
gained a university education (without degree award) in the
natural sciences before her early death at the age of thirty-one,
satirized men's treatment of educated 'New Women', that is,
women who had emancipated themselves from the shackles of
passive 'femininity' and frivolity. In Naden's lively poem, 'Love
Versus Learning' (1881), the female narrator discovers that her
educated lover lacks intellectual passion:

> He says that my lips are too rosy
>   To speak in a language that's dead,
> And all that is dismal and prosy
>   Should fly from so sunny a head.
>
> He scoffs at each grave occupation,
>   Turns everything off with a pun;
> And says that his sole calculation
>   Is how to make two into one.

The narrator's sexual joke belies the seriousness of this satirical
poem in which women's battles against sexism in education can

be seen to have originated in the previous century. Dollie Radford also, in 'From Our Emancipated Aunt in Town' (1895), writes witty verse about the difficulties that the 'New Woman' encountered:

> The fairy prince has passed from sight,
> Away into the ewigkeit,
>   With best intention
>   . . .
>
> And though he's only left to me,
> Of course quite inadvertently,
>   The faintest glimmer
>
> Of humour, to illume my way,
> I'm thankful he has had his day,
>   His shine and shimmer.

The narrator humorously puts paid to the notion of 'Prince Charming' or 'Mr Right'. Yet up till now these witty subversive poems by Naden and Radford, which deconstruct notions of the ideal male lover, have not been available to readers.

Several of these women poets show verve and originality in tackling social topics which were at that time coming to the fore and which are still relevant. Eliza Cook's 'Song of the Spirit of Poverty' (1845) is as pertinent in today's world as in early Victorian England, and Janet Hamilton's Scottish dialogue in 'Rhymes for the Times' (1863) both satirizes male opponents of women's emancipation and sermonizes about women's duties in maintaining female traditions. On the subject of married women's new legal rights to own and retain their own property, Moira O'Neill's humorous literary ballad, 'The Grand Match' (1900) shows how the stereotypical male fortune-seeker, who marries a prosperous farmer's daughter for money instead of love, gets his come-uppance; he is unable to assert power over her as he might have done earlier in the century, and is forced to endure 'the tongue o' the woman that owns him'. Even on the subject of animal rights, Dora Greenwell's ballad 'Fidelity Rewarded' (1889) should touch a chord in those readers who question the use of animals in scientific experiments.

A variety of forms and diction characterize the poetry of these Victorian women poets. Augusta Webster and Amy Levy were among those who tried out the dramatic monologue that Robert Browning had used so successfully. And, although many of them fell back on the simple quatrain, most of these poets could achieve a well-turned sonnet, the form re-introduced into English poetry in the Romantic period by Charlotte Smith. The sonnet sequences of Elizabeth Barrett Browning, Christina Rossetti and Augusta Webster are strikingly original in their imaginative reversals of the themes of men's 'love' sonnets. But what is even more striking is the way in which women poets, such as Amy Levy, Constance Naden, Dora Sigerson, Dora Greenwell and others, began to use colloquial rather than elevated language in their poems as a matter of course, a fact which makes their work eminently readable to-day.

If readers and writers are to be enabled to explore and understand a women's tradition of Victorian poetry, we need to have access to representative works from the entire period. This anthology gives some prominence of course to those few women poets, such as Elizabeth Barrett Browning and Christina Rossetti, who have been accepted in the male 'canon'. But remarkable poets such as Constance Naden and Mary Elizabeth Coleridge, who deserve a place in any so-called 'canon', are also featured here. In addition, readers will discover a wide range of poets such as Mathilde Blind, Dora Greenwell, Jean Ingelow and others who, among their reams of once popular versifying, wrote a few poems which remain of interest today. The reading of a full range of women's poetry from the period, with its variety of preoccupations, enhances our appreciation of this women's tradition and expands our understanding of Victorian poetry.

JENNIFER BREEN

NOTES

1 John Feather, *A History of British Publishing*, Chs. 11–12, Routledge, 1988, pp. 129–49.

2 R. G. Alston, 'Introduction', *A Checklist of Women Writers. 1801–1900: Fiction Verse Drama*, The British Library, 1990, pp. viii–ix. For bibliographical and biographical dictionaries which give information about Victorian women writers, see individual entries in *The Feminist Companion to Literature in English: Women Writers from the Middle Ages to the Present*, ed. Virginia Blain, Patricia Clements, and Isobel Grundy (1990) and *A Dictionary of Women Writers*, ed. Janet Todd (1989).

3 John Stuart Mill, *The Subjection of Women*, reprinted in *Essays on Sex Equality*, ed. Alice S. Rossi, University of Chicago Press, 1970, pp. 147–8.

4 Mary Wollstonecraft, *A Vindication of the Rights of Woman*, 2nd edn, 1792, reprinted in *The Works of Mary Wollstonecraft*, ed. Janet Todd and Marilyn Butler, Vol. 5, London, Pickering & Chatto, p. 189.

5 Gail Braybon & Penny Summerfield, *Out of the Cage: Women's Experiences in Two World Wars*, Routledge, 1987, p. 150.

6 'Introduction', *Reform and Intellectual Debate in Victorian England*, ed. Barbara Dennis & David Skilton, Kent, Croom Helm, 1987, pp. 15–17.

7 Michael Sanderson, *Educational Opportunity and Social Change in England*, Faber, 1987, p. 44, and Braybon & Summerfield, p. 138.

8 Braybon & Summerfield, pp. 11 and 20.

9 See Julia Swindells, *Victorian Writing and Working Women: The Other Side of Silence* (London, Polity Press, 1985).

10 Martha Vicinus, *The Industrial Muse: A Study of Nineteenth-Century British Working-Class Literature*, Croom Helm, 1974, pp. 117–18 and 161.

11 Christina Rossetti, *The Poetical Works*, ed. W. M. Rossetti, 1904, p. 50.

NOTE ON THE TEXT

These poems are printed, with a few exceptions, from the authors' first editions in book form. These women poets are arranged here in chronological order according to the date of each author's first poem included in this anthology. The poems by each author are printed in chronological order of date of first publication. This date appears at the end of each poem. Sources for these poems are given in the biographical and explanatory Notes for individual authors, which are arranged, for convenient reference, in alphabetical order.

VICTORIAN
WOMEN POETS
An Anthology

CAROLINE NORTON

My Heart Is Like a Withered Nut

My heart is like a withered nut,
  Rattling within its hollow shell;
You cannot open my breast, and put
  Anything fresh with it to dwell.
The hopes and dreams that filled it when
  Life's spring of glory met my view,
Are gone! and ne'er with joy or pain
  That shrunken heart shall swell anew.

My heart is like a withered nut;
  Once it was soft to every touch,   10
But now 'tis stern and closely shut—
  I would not have to plead with such.
Each light-toned voice once cleared my brow,
  Each gentle breeze once shook the tree
Where hung the sun-lit fruit, which now
  Lies cold, and stiff, and sad, like me!

My heart is like a withered nut—
  It once was comely to the view;
But since misfortune's blast hath cut,
  It hath a dark and mournful hue.   20
The freshness of its verdant youth
  Nought to that fruit can now restore;
And my poor heart, I feel in truth,
  Nor sun, nor smile shall light it more.

1830

I Was Not False to Thee

I was not false to *thee*, and yet,
My cheek alone looked pale;
My weary eye was dim and wet,
My strength began to fail.
Thou wert the same; thy looks were gay,
Thy step was light and free;
And yet, with truth, my heart can say,
I was not false to *thee*!

I was not false to thee, yet now
Thou hast a cheerful eye,
With flushing cheek and drooping brow
I wander mournfully.
I hate to meet the gaze of men,
I weep where none can see;
Why do *I* only suffer, when
I was not false to *thee*?

I was not false to thee; yet oh!
How scornfully they smile,
Who see me droop, who guess my woe,
Yet court thee all the while.
'Tis strange! but when long years are past,
Thou wilt remember me;
Whilst I can feel until the last,
I was not false to *thee*!

1830

Sonnet 4

Be frank with me, and I accept my lot;
    But deal not with me as a grieving child,
Who for the loss of that which he hath not
    Is by a show of kindness thus beguiled.
Raise not for me, from its enshrouded tomb,
    The ghostly likeness of a hope deceased;

Nor think to cheat the darkness of my doom
  By wavering doubts how far thou art released:
This dressing pity in the garb of Love,
  This effort of the heart to *seem* the same,—   10
These sighs and lingerings, (which nothing prove
  But that thou leavest me with a kind of shame,)—
Remind me more, by their most vain deceit,
Of the dear loss of all which thou dost counterfeit.

1840

Sonnet 5

Because I know that there is that in me
  Of which thou shouldst be proud, and not ashamed,—
Because I feel one made *thy* choice should be
  Not even by fools and slanderers rashly blamed,—
Because I fear, howe'er thy soul may strive
  Against the weakness of that inward pain,
The falsehoods which my enemies contrive
  Not always seek to wound thine ear in vain,—
Therefore I sometimes weep, when I should smile,
  At all the vain frivolity and sin   10
Which those who know me not (yet me revile)—
  My would-be judges—cast my actions in;
But else their malice hath nor sting nor smart—
For I appeal from them, Beloved, to thine own heart!

1840

CHARLOTTE BRONTË

Presentiment

'Sister, you've sat there all the day,
  Come to the hearth awhile;
The wind so wildly sweeps away,
  The clouds so darkly pile.
That open book has lain, unread,
  For hours upon your knee;
You've never smiled nor turned your head;
  What can you, sister, see?'

'Come hither, Jane, look down the field;
  How dense a mist creeps on!   1
The path, the hedge, are both concealed,
  Even the white gate is gone;
No landscape through the fog I trace,
  No hill with pastures green;
All featureless is Nature's face,
  All masked in clouds her mien.

'Scarce is the rustle of a leaf
  Heard in our garden now;
The year grows old, its days wax brief,
  The tresses leave its brow.   2
The rain drives fast before the wind,
  The sky is blank and grey;
O Jane, what sadness fills the mind
  On such a dreary day!'

'You think too much, my sister dear;
  You sit too long alone;
What though November days be drear?
  Full soon they will be gone.
I've swept the hearth, and placed your chair,
  Come, Emma, sit by me;   3

Our own fireside is never drear,
Though late and wintry wanes the year,
   Though rough the night may be.'

'The peaceful glow of our fireside
   Imparts no peace to me:
My thoughts would rather wander wide
   Than rest, dear Jane, with thee.
I'm on a distant journey bound,
   And if, about my heart,
Too closely kindred ties were bound,   40
   'Twould break when forced to part.

' "Soon will November days be o'er"—
   Well have you spoken, Jane:
My own forebodings tell me more—
For me, I know by presage sure,
   They'll ne'er return again.
Ere long, nor sun nor storm to me
   Will bring or joy or gloom;
They reach not that Eternity
   Which soon will be my home.'   50
                *   *   *
Eight months are gone, the summer sun
   Sets in a glorious sky;
A quiet field, all green and lone,
   Receives its rosy dye.
Jane sits upon a shaded stile,
   Alone she sits there now;
Her head rests on her hand the while
   And thought o'ercasts her brow.

She's thinking of one winter's day,
   A few short months ago,   60
When Emma's bier was borne away
   O'er wastes of frozen snow.
She's thinking how that drifted snow
   Dissolved in spring's first gleam,
And how her sister's memory now
   Fades, even as fades a dream.

The snow will whiten earth again,
    But Emma comes no more;
She left, 'mid winter's sleet and rain,
    This world for Heaven's far shore.   70
On Beulah's hills she wanders now,
    On Eden's tranquil plain;
To her shall Jane hereafter go,*
    She ne'er shall come to Jane!

1837

The Teacher's Monologue

The room is quiet, thoughts alone
    People its mute tranquillity;
The yoke put off, the long task done,—
    I am, as it is bliss to be,
Still and untroubled. Now, I see,
    For the first time, how soft the day
O'er waveless water, stirless tree,
    Silent and sunny, wings its way.
Now, as I watch that distant hill,
    So faint, so blue, so far removed,   10
Sweet dreams of home my heart may fill,
    That home where I am known and loved:
It lies beyond; yon azure brow
    Parts me from all Earth holds for me;
And, morn and eve, my yearnings flow
    Thitherward tending, changelessly.
My happiest hours, ay! all the time,
    I love to keep in memory,
Lapsed among moors, ere life's first prime
    Decayed to dark anxiety.   20

Sometimes, I think a narrow heart
    Makes me thus mourn those far away,
And keeps my love so far apart
    From friends and friendships of today;

Sometimes, I think 'tis but a dream
  I treasure up so jealously,
All the sweet thoughts I live on seem
  To vanish into vacancy:
And then, this strange, coarse world around
  Seems all that's palpable and true;   30
And every sight and every sound
  Combines my spirit to subdue
To aching grief; so void and lone
  Is Life and Earth—so worse than vain,
The hopes that, in my own heart sown,
  And cherished by such sun and rain
As Joy and transient Sorrow shed,
  Have ripened to a harvest there:
Alas! methinks I hear it said,
  'Thy golden sheaves are empty air.'   40
All fades away; my very home
  I think will soon be desolate;
I hear, at times, a warning come
  Of bitter partings at its gate;
And, if I should return and see
  The hearth-fire quenched, the vacant chair;
And hear it whispered mournfully,
  That farewells have been spoken there,
What shall I do, and whither turn?
Where look for peace? When cease to mourn?   50
      *   *   *
'Tis not the air I wished to play,
  The strain I wished to sing;
My wilful spirit slipped away
  And struck another string.
I neither wanted smile nor tear,
  Bright joy nor bitter woe,
But just a song that sweet and clear,
  Though haply sad, might flow.

A quiet song, to solace me
  When sleep refused to come;   60
A strain to chase despondency
  When sorrowful for home.

In vain I try; I cannot sing;
   All feels so cold and dead;
No wild distress, no gushing spring
   Of tears in anguish shed;

But all the impatient gloom of one
   Who waits a distant day,
When, some great task of suffering done,
   Repose shall toil repay.   70
For youth departs, and pleasure flies,
   And life consumes away,
And youth's rejoicing ardour dies
   Beneath this drear delay;

And Patience, weary with her yoke,
   Is yielding to despair,
And Health's elastic spring is broke
   Beneath the strain of care.
Life will be gone ere I have lived;
   Where now is Life's first prime?   80
I've worked and studied, longed and grieved,
Through all that rosy time.

To toil, to think, to long, to grieve,—
   Is such my future fate?
The morn was dreary, must the eve
   Be also desolate?
Well, such a life at least makes Death
   A welcome, wished-for friend;
Then, aid me, Reason, Patience, Faith,
   To suffer to the end!   90

1837

Stanzas

If thou be in a lonely place
   If one hour's calm be thine,
As Evening bends her placid face
   O'er this sweet day's decline;

If all the earth and all the heaven
   Now look serene to thee,
As o'er them shuts the summer even,
   One moment—think of me!

Pause, in the lane, returning home;
   'Tis dusk, it will be still: 10
Pause, near the elm, a sacred gloom
   Its breezeless boughs will fill.
Look at that soft and golden light,
   High in the unclouded sky;
Watch the last bird's belated flight,
   As it flits silent by.

Hark! for a sound upon the wind,
   A step, a voice, a sigh;
If all be still, then yield thy mind,
   Unchecked, to memory.   20
If thy love were like mine, how blest
   That twilight hour would seem,
When, back from the regretted Past,
   Returned our early dream!

If thy love were like mine, how wild
   Thy longings, even to pain,
For sunset soft, and moonlight mild,
   To bring that hour again!
But oft, when in thine arms I lay,
   I've seen thy dark eyes shine,   30
And deeply felt their changeful ray
   Spoke other love than mine.

My love is almost anguish now,
   It beats so strong and true;
'Twere rapture, could I deem that thou
   Such anguish ever knew.
I have been but thy transient flower,
   Thou wert my god divine;
Till checked by death's congealing power,
   This heart must throb for thine.   40

And well my dying hour were blest,
   If life's expiring breath
Should pass, as thy lips gently prest
   My forehead cold in death;
And sound my sleep would be, and sweet,
   Beneath the churchyard tree,
If sometimes in thy heart should beat
   One pulse, still true to me.

1837

'The Autumn day its course has run . . .'

The Autumn day its course has run
   The Autumn evening falls,
Already risen the Autumn moon
   Gleams quiet on these walls.

And twilight to my lonely house
   A silent guest is come:
In mask of gloom, through every room
   She passes dusk and dumb.

Her veil is spread, her shadows shed
   O'er stair and chamber void,
And now I feel her presence steal
   Even to my lone fireside.

                                      10

Sit, silent Nun—sit here and be
Comrade and confidante to me.

1843

'Early wrapt in slumber deep . . .'

Early wrapt in slumber deep
   Rest the serving-men;
Master, dame, and hand-maid sleep
   Sound, at Bonny glen.

Time's dark stream, in yonder vales,
  Glides with shadowed flow;
O'er each latticed window falls
  A drapery, sweeping low.

While, within the house, is spread
  Shade o'er weary eyes,   10
Screenless, in his out-door shed,
  A little herd-boy lies.

Splendid light from summer moon
  Falls on each green tree;
Soft as twilight, clear as noon,
  Smiles each dewy lea.

Water in the clear brook flows
  Fast, with trembling brightness;
By its side, the causeway shows
  A track of silver whiteness.   20

1843

Lost in the Hills

I now had only to retrace
  The long and lonely road
So lately in the rainbow chase
  With fearless ardour trod.

Behind, I left the sunshine, now
  The evening setting sun,
Before, a storm rolled dark and low
  Some gloomy hills upon.

It came with rain—it came with wind,
  With swollen stream it howled,   10
And night advancing black and blind
  In ebon horror scowled.

Lost in the hills—all painfully
  I climbed a heathy peak,
I sought, I longed afar to see
  My life's light's parting streak.

The West was black as if no day
  Had ever lingered there,
As if no red, expiring ray
  Had tinged the enkindled air.   20

And morning's portals could not lie
  Where yon dark Orient spread:
The funeral North—the black dark sky
  Alike mourned for the dead.

1846

The North Wind*

That wind is from the North: I know it well;
No other breeze could have so wild a swell.
Now deep and loud it thunders round my cell,
    Then faintly dies, and softly sighs,
And moans and murmurs mournfully.
I know its language; thus it speaks to me;

'I have passed over thy own mountains dear,
Thy northern mountains, and they still are free;
Still lonely, wild, majestic, bleak, and drear,
    And stern, and lovely, as they used to be   10

'When thou, a young enthusiast,
    As wild and free as they,
O'er rocks, and glens, and snowy heights,
    Didst often love to stray.

'I've blown the pure, untrodden snows
    In whirling eddies from their brows;
And I have howled in caverns wild,
Where thou, a joyous mountain-child,
    Didst dearly love to be.
The sweet world is not changed, but thou   20
Art pining in a dungeon now,
    Where thou must ever be.

'No voice but mine can reach thy ear,
And Heaven has kindly sent me here
    To mourn and sigh with thee,
And tell thee of the cherished land
    Of thy nativity.'

Blow on, wild wind; thy solemn voice,
    However sad and drear,
Is nothing to the gloomy silence   30
    I have had to bear.

Hot tears are streaming from my eyes,
    But these are better far
Than that dull, gnawing, tearless time,
    The stupor of despair.

Confined and hopeless as I am,
    Oh, speak of liberty!
Oh, tell me of my mountain home,
    And I will welcome thee!

                    1838

Lines Written at Thorp Green*

That summer sun, whose genial glow
Now cheers my drooping spirit so,
    Must cold and silent be,
And only light our northern clime
With feeble ray, before the time
    I long so much to see.

And this soft whispering breeze, that now
So gently cools my fevered brow,
    This too, alas! must turn
To a wild blast, whose icy dart
Pierces and chills me to the heart,
    Before I cease to mourn.   10

And these bright flowers I love so well,
Verbena, rose, and sweet bluebell,
    Must droop and die away;
Those thick, green leaves, with all their shade
And rustling music, they must fade,
    And every one decay.

But if the sunny, summer time,
And woods and meadows in their prime,
  Are sweet to them that roam;
Far sweeter is the winter bare,   20
With long, dark nights, and landscape drear,
  To them that are at Home!

1841

Appeal*

  Oh, I am very weary,
    Though tears no longer flow;
My eyes are tired of weeping,
    My heart is sick of woe;

  My life is very lonely,
    My days pass heavily,
I'm weary of repining;
    Wilt thou not come to me?

  Oh, didst thou know my longings
    For thee, from day to day,   10
My hopes, so often blighted,
    Thou wouldst not thus delay!

1841

The Captive Dove

Poor restless dove, I pity thee;
  And when I hear thy plaintive moan,
I mourn for thy captivity,
  And in thy woes forget mine own.

To see thee stand prepared to fly,
  And flap those useless wings of thine,
And gaze into the distant sky,
  Would melt a harder heart than mine.

In vain—in vain! Thou canst not rise;
    Thy prison roof confines thee there;   10
Its slender wires delude thine eyes,
    And quench thy longings with despair.

Oh, thou wert made to wander free
    In sunny mead and shady grove,
And far beyond the rolling sea,
    In distant climes, at will to rove!

Yet, hadst thou but one gentle mate
    Thy little drooping heart to cheer,
And share with thee thy captive state,
    Thou couldst be happy even there.   20

Yes, even there, if, listening by,
    One faithful dear companion stood;
While gazing on her full bright eye,
    Thou mightst forget thy native wood.

But thou, poor solitary dove,
    Must make, unheard, thy joyless moan;
The heart that Nature formed to love
    Must pine, neglected, and alone.

1843

Night

I love the silent hour of night,
    For blissful dreams may then arise,
Revealing to my charmèd sight
    What may not bless my waking eyes.

And then a voice may meet my ear,
    That death has silenced long ago;
And hope and rapture may appear
    Instead of solitude and woe.

Cold in the grave for years has lain
   The form it was my bliss to see;   10
And only dreams can bring again
   The darling of my heart to me.

1845

The Arbour

I'll rest me in this sheltered bower,
   And look upon the clear blue sky
That smiles upon me through the trees,
   Which stand so thickly clustering by;

And view their green and glossy leaves,
   All glistening in the sunshine fair;
And list the rustling of their boughs,
   So softly whispering through the air.

And while my ear drinks in the sound,
   My wingèd soul shall fly away;   10
Reviewing long departed years
   As one mild, beaming, autumn day;

And soaring on to future scenes,
   Like hills and woods, and valleys green,
All basking in the summer's sun,
   But distant still, and dimly seen.

Oh, list! 'tis summer's very breath
   That gently shakes the rustling trees—
But look! the snow is on the ground—
   How can I think of scenes like these?   20

'Tis but the *frost* that clears the air,
   And gives the sky that lovely blue;
They're smiling in the *winter's* sun,
   Those evergreens of sombre hue.

And winter's chill is on my heart—
   How can I dream of future bliss?
How can my spirit soar away,
   Confined by such a chain as this?

c. 1845

Domestic Peace*

Why should such gloomy silence reign,
   And why is all the house so drear,
When neither danger, sickness, pain,
   Nor death, nor want, has entered here?

We are as many as we were
   That other night, when all were gay
And full of hope, and free from care;
   Yet is there something gone away.

The moon without, as pure and calm,
   Is shining as that night she shone;   10
But now, to us, she brings no balm,
   For something from our hearts is gone.

Something whose absence leaves a void—
   A cheerless want in every heart;
Each feels the bliss of all destroyed,
   And mourns the change—but each apart.

The fire is burning in the grate
   As redly as it used to burn;
But still the hearth is desolate,
   Till mirth, and love, with *peace* return.   20

'Twas *peace* that flowed from heart to heart,
   With looks and smiles that spoke of heaven,
And gave us language to impart
   The blissful thoughts itself had given.

Domestic peace! best joy of earth,
 When shall we all thy value learn?
White angel, to our sorrowing hearth,
 Return,—oh, graciously return!

1846

EMILY BRONTË

Hope

Hope was but a timid friend;
   She sat without the grated den,
Watching how my fate would tend,
   Even as selfish-hearted men.

She was cruel in her fear;
   Through the bars, one dreary day,
I looked out to see her there,
   And she turned her face away!

Like a false guard, false watch keeping,
   Still, in strife, she whispered peace;   10
She would sing while I was weeping;
   If I listened, she would cease.

False she was, and unrelenting;
   When my last joys strewed the ground,
Even Sorrow saw, repenting,
   Those sad relics scattered round;

Hope, whose whisper would have given
   Balm to all my frenzied pain,
Stretched her wings, and soared to heaven,
   Went, and ne'er returned again!   20

1843

Song

The linnet in the rocky dells,
   The moor-lark in the air,
The bee among the heather bells
   That hide my lady fair:

The wild deer browse above her breast;
 The wild birds raise their brood;
And they, her smiles of love caressed,
 Have left her solitude!

I ween, that when the grave's dark wall
 Did first her form retain,   10
They thought their hearts could ne'er recall
 The light of joy again.

They thought the tide of grief would flow
 Unchecked through future years;
But where is all their anguish now,
 And where are all their tears?

Well, let them fight for honour's breath,
 Or pleasure's shade pursue—
The dweller in the land of death
 Is changed and careless too.   20

And, if their eyes should watch and weep
 Till sorrow's source were dry,
She would not, in her tranquil sleep,
 Return a single sigh!

Blow, west-wind, by the lonely mound,
 And murmur, summer-streams—
There is no need of other sound
 To soothe my lady's dreams.

1844

To Imagination

When weary with the long day's care,
 And earthly change from pain to pain,
And lost, and ready to despair,
 Thy kind voice calls me back again,

O my true friend! I am not lone,
While thou canst speak with such a tone!

So hopeless is the world without,
   The world within I doubly prize;
Thy world, where guile, and hate, and doubt
   And cold suspicion never rise;   10
Where thou, and I, and Liberty,
Have undisputed sovereignty.

What matters it, that all around
   Danger, and guilt, and darkness lie,
If but within our bosom's bound
   We hold a bright, untroubled sky,
Warm with ten thousand mingled rays
Of suns that know no winter days?

Reason, indeed, may oft complain
   For Nature's sad reality,   20
And tell the suffering heart how vain
   Its cherished dreams must always be;
And Truth may rudely trample down
The flowers of Fancy, newly-blown:

But thou are ever there, to bring
   The hovering vision back, and breathe
New glories o'er the blighted spring,
   And call a lovelier Life from Death,
And whisper, with a voice divine,
Of real worlds, as bright as thine.   30

I trust not to thy phantom bliss,
   Yet, still, in evening's quiet hour,
With never-failing thankfulness,
   I welcome thee, Benignant Power,
Sure solacer of human cares,
And sweeter hope, when hope despairs!

1844

Faith and Despondency*

'The winter wind is loud and wild:
Come close to me, my darling child;
Forsake thy books, and mateless play,
And, while the night is gathering grey,
We'll talk its pensive hours away.

'Ierne, round our sheltered hall
November's gusts unheeded call;
Not one faint breath can enter here
Enough to wave my daughter's hair;
And I am glad to watch the blaze   10
Glance from her eyes with mimic rays;
To feel her cheek so softly pressed,
In happy quiet on my breast.

'But, yet, even this tranquillity
Brings bitter, restless thoughts to me;
And, in the red fire's cheerful glow,
I think of deep glens, blocked with snow;
I dream of moor, and misty hill,
Where evening closes dark and chill;
For, lone, among the mountains cold   20
Lie those that I have loved of old.
And my heart aches, in hopeless pain,
Exhausted with repinings vain,
That I shall greet them ne'er again!'

'Father, in early infancy,
When you were far beyond the sea,
Such thoughts were tyrants over me!
I often sat, for hours together,
Through the long nights of angry weather,   30
Raised on my pillow, to descry
The dim moon struggling in the sky;
Or, with strained ear, to catch the shock,
Of rock with wave, and wave with rock;
So would I fearful vigil keep,
And, all for listening, never sleep.

But this world's life has much to dread:
Not so, my father, with the dead.

'Oh! not for them should we despair,
The grave is drear, but they are not here: 40
Their dust is mingled with the sod;
Their happy souls are gone to God!
You told me this, and yet you sigh,
And murmur that your friends must die.
Ah! my dear father, tell me why?
For, if your former words were true,
    How useless would such sorrow be!
As wise, to mourn the seed which grew
    Unnoticed on its parent tree,
Because it fell in fertile earth,   50
And sprang up to a glorious birth—
Struck deep its root and lifted high
Its green boughs in the breezy sky.

'But I'll not fear: I will not weep
For those whose bodies rest in sleep,
I know there is a blessed shore,
    Opening its port for me and mine;
And, gazing Time's wide waters o'er,
    I weary for that land divine,
Where we were born, where you and I   60
Shall meet our dearest, when we die;
From suffering and corruption free,
Restored into the Deity.'

'Well hast thou spoken, sweet, trustful child!
    And wiser than thy sire;
And worldly tempests, raging wild,
    Shall strengthen thy desire—
Thy fervent hope, through storm and foam,
To reach, at last, the eternal home,
    The steadfast, changeless shore!'   70

1844

*Remembrance**

Cold in the earth—and the deep snow piled above thee,
   Far, far removed, cold in the dreary grave!
Have I forgot, my only Love, to love thee,
   Severed at last by Time's all-severing wave?

Now, when alone, do my thoughts no longer hover
   Over the mountains, on that northern shore,
Resting their wings where heath and fern-leaves cover
   Thy noble heart for ever, ever more?

Cold in the earth—and fifteen wild Decembers*
   From those brown hills, have melted into spring: 10
Faithful, indeed, is the spirit that remembers
   After such years of change and suffering!

Sweet Love of youth, forgive, if I forget thee,
   While the world's tide is bearing me along;
Other desires and other hopes beset me,
   Hopes which obscure, but cannot do thee wrong!

No later light has lightened up my heaven,
   No second morn has ever shone for me;
All my life's bliss from thy dear life was given,
   All my life's bliss is in the grave with thee.   20

But when the days of golden dreams had perished,
   And even Despair was powerless to destroy,
Then did I learn how existence could be cherished,
   Strengthened, and fed, without the aid of joy.

Then did I check the tears of useless passion
   Weaned my young soul from yearning after thine;
Sternly denied its burning wish to hasten
   Down to that tomb already more than mine.

And, even yet, I dare not let it languish,
   Dare not indulge in memory's rapturous pain;   30
Once drinking deep of that divinest anguish,
   How could I seek the empty world again?

1845

The Philosopher

Enough of thought, philosopher!
   Too long hast thou been dreaming
Unlightened, in this chamber drear,
   While summer's sun is beaming!
Space-sweeping soul, what sad refrain
Concludes thy musings once again?

'Oh, for the time when I shall sleep
   Without identity,
And never care how rain may steep,
   Or snow may cover me!   10
No promised heaven, these wild desires
   Could all or half fulfil;
No threatened hell, with quenchless fires,
   Subdue this quenchless will!'

'So said I, and still say the same;
   Still, to my death, will say—
Three gods, within this little frame,
   Are warring, night and day;
Heaven could not hold them all, and yet
   They all are held in me;   20
And must be mine till I forget
   My present entity!
Oh, for the time, when in my breast
   Their struggles will be o'er!
Oh, for the day, when I shall rest,
   And never suffer more!'

'I saw a spirit, standing, man,
   Where thou dost stand—an hour ago,

And round his feet three rivers ran,
  Of equal depth, and equal flow—   30
A golden stream—and one like blood;
  And one like sapphire seemed to be;
But where they joined their triple flood
  It tumbled in an inky sea.
The spirit sent his dazzling gaze
  Down through that ocean's gloomy night;
Then, kindling all, with sudden blaze,
  The glad deep sparkled wide and bright—
White as the sun, far, far more fair
  Than its divided sources were!'   40

'And even for that spirit, seer,
  I've watched and sought my lifetime long;
Sought him in heaven, hell, earth, and air,
  And endless search, and always wrong.
Had I but seen his glorious eye
  Once light the clouds that 'wilder me,
I ne'er had raised this coward cry
  To cease to think, and cease to be;
I ne'er had called oblivion blest,
  Nor, stretching eager hands to death,   50
Implored to change for senseless rest
  This sentient soul, this living breath,
Oh, let me die—that power and will
  Their cruel strife may close;
And conquered good and conquering ill
  Be lost in one repose!'

                                    1845

No Coward Soul Is Mine

  No coward soul is mine,
No trembler in the world's storm-troubled sphere:
  I see Heaven's glories shine,
And Faith shines equal, arming me from Fear.

O God within my breast,
Almighty, ever-present Deity!
    Life, that in me has rest,
As I, undying Life, have power in Thee!

    Vain are the thousand creeds
That move men's hearts: unutterably vain;   10
    Worthless as withered weeds,
Or idlest froth amid the boundless main,

    To waken doubt in one
Holding so fast by Thy infinity,
    So surely anchored on
The steadfast rock of Immortality.

    With wide-embracing love
Thy Spirit animates eternal years,
    Pervades and broods above,
Changes, sustains, dissolves, creates, and rears.   20

    Though earth and moon were gone,
And suns and universes ceased to be,
    And Thou wert left alone,
Every existence would exist in Thee.

    There is not room for Death,
Nor atom that his might could render void:
    Thou—Thou art Being and Breath,
And what Thou art may never be destroyed.

                    1846

Sonnet

Whene'er I recollect the happy time
When you and I held converse dear together,
There come a thousand thoughts of sunny weather,
Of early blossoms, and the fresh year's prime;
Your memory lives forever in my mind
With all the fragrant beauties of the spring
With odorous lime and silver hawthorn twined,
And many a noonday woodland wandering.
There's not a thought of you, but brings along
Some sunny dream of river, field, and sky;   10
'Tis wafted on the blackbird's sunset song,
Or some wild snatch of ancient melody.
And as I date it still, our love arose
'Twixt the last violet and the earliest rose.

1844

Sonnet

I hear a voice low in the sunset woods;
    Listen, it says: 'Decay, decay, decay!'
I hear it in the murmuring of the floods,
    And the wind sighs it as it flies away.
Autumn is come; seest thou not in the skies,
The stormy light of his fierce lurid eyes?
Autumn is come; his brazen feet have trod,
Withering and scorching, o'er the mossy sod.
The fainting year sees her fresh flowery wreath
Shrivel in his hot grasp; his burning breath   10
Dries the sweet water-springs that in the shade

Wandering along, delicious music made.
A flood of glory hangs upon the world,
Summer's bright wings shining ere they are furled.

1844

Song of the Spirit of Poverty

A song, a song for the beldam Queen,
    A Queen that the world knows well,
Whose portal of state is the workhouse gate,
    And throne the prison cell.

I have been crowned in every land
    With nightshade steeped in tears,
I've a dog-gnawn bone for my sceptre wand,
    Which the proudest mortal fears.

No gem I wear in my tangled hair,
    No golden vest I own,   10
No radiant glow tints cheek or brow,
    Yet say, who dares my frown?

Oh, I am Queen of a ghastly court,
    And tyrant sway I hold,
Baiting human hearts for my royal sport
    With the bloodhounds of Hunger and Cold.

My power can change the purest clay
    From its first and beautiful mould,
Till it hideth from the face of day,
    Too hideous to behold.   20

Mark ye the wretch who has cloven and cleft
    The skull of the lonely one,
And quailed not at purpling his blade to the heft,
    To make sure that the deed was done:

Fair seeds were sown in his infant breast,
    That held goodly blossom and fruit,
But I trampled them down—Man did the rest—
    And God's image grew into the brute.

He hath been driven, and hunted, and scourged,
   For the sin I bade him do,   30
He hath wrought the lawless work I urged,
   Till blood seemed fair to his view.

I shriek with delight to see him bedight
   In fetters that chink and gleam;
'He is mine!' I shout, as they lead him out
   From the dungeon to the beam.

See the lean boy clutch his rough-hewn crutch,
   With limbs all warped and worn,
While hurries along through a noisy throng
   The theme of their gibing scorn.   40

Wealth and care would have reared him straight
   As the towering mountain pine,
But I nursed him into that halting gait,
   And withered his marrowless spine.

Pain may be heard on the downy bed,
   Heaving the groan of despair,
For Suffering shuns not the diademed head,
   And abideth everywhere.

But the shortened breath and parching lip
   Are watched by many an eye,   50
And there is a balmy drink to sip,
   And tender hands to ply.

Come, come with me, and ye shall see
   What a child of mine can bear,
Where squalid shadows thicken the light,
   And foulness taints the air.

He lieth alone to gasp and moan,
   While the cancer eats his flesh,
With the old rags festering on his wound,
   For none will give him fresh.   60

Oh, carry him forth in a blanket robe,
  The lazar-house is nigh,
The careless hand shall cut and probe,
  And strangers see him die.

Where's the escutcheon of blazoned worth?
  Who is heir to the famed rich man?
Ha! ha! he is mine—dig a hole in the earth,
  And hide him as soon as ye can.

Oh, I am Queen of a ghastly Court,
  And the handmaids that I keep   70
Are such phantom things as Fever brings
  To haunt the fitful sleep.

See, see, they come in my haggard train,
  With jagged and matted locks
Hanging round them as rough as the wild steed's mane,
  Or the black weed on the rocks.

They come with broad and horny palms,
  They come in maniac guise,
With angled chins, and yellow skins,
  And hollow staring eyes.   80

They come to be girded with leather and link,
  And away at my bidding they go,
To toil where the soulless beast would shrink,
  In the deep, damp caverns below.

Daughters of beauty, they, like ye,
  Are of gentle womankind—
And wonder not if little there be
  Of angel form and mind:

If I'd held your cheeks by as close a pinch,
  Would that flourishing rose be found?   90
If I'd doled you a crust out, inch by inch,
  Would your arms have been so round?

Oh, I am Queen with a despot rule,
    That crushes to the dust;
The laws I deal bear no appeal,
    Though ruthless and unjust.

I deaden the bosom and darken the brain,
    With the might of the demon's skill;
The heart may struggle, but struggle in vain,
    As I grapple it harder still.   100

Oh, come with me, and ye shall see
    How well I begin the day,
For I'll hie to the hungriest slave I have,
    And snatch his loaf away.

Oh, come with me, and ye shall see
    How my skeleton victims fall;
How I order the graves without a stone,
    And the coffins without a pall.

Then a song, a song for the beldam Queen—
    A Queen that ye fear right well;   110
For my portal of state is the workhouse gate,
    And my throne the prison cell.

1845

MARY HOWITT

The Barley-Mowers' Song

Barley-mowers here we stand,
One, two, three, a steady band;
True of heart and strong of limb,
Ready in our harvest-trim;
All arow, with spirits blithe,
Now we whet the bended scythe.
    Rink-a-tink, rink-a-tink, rink-a-tink-a-tink!

Side by side now, bending low,
Down the swaths of barley go;
Stroke by stroke, as true as chime   10
Of the bells we keep in time:
Then we whet the ringing scythe,
Standing 'mid the barley lithe.
    Rink-a-tink, rink-a-tink, rink-a-tink-a-tink!

After labour cometh ease;
Sitting now beneath the trees,
Round we send the barley-wine,
Life-infusing, clear and fine;
Then refreshed, alert and blithe,
Rise we all, and whet the scythe.   20
    Rink-a-tink, rink-a-tink, rink-a-tink-a-tink!

Barley-mowers must be true,
Keeping still the end in view;
One with all, and all with one,
Working on till set of sun;
Bending all with spirits blithe,
Whetting all at once the scythe.
    Rink-a-tink, rink-a-tink, rink-a-tink-a-tink!

Day and night, and night and day,
Time the mower, will not stay: 30
We may hear him in our path
By the falling barley-swath;
While we sing with spirits blithe,
We may hear his ringing scythe.
   Rink-a-tink, rink-a-tink, rink-a-tink-a-tink!

Time the mower cuts down all,
High and low, and great and small:
Fear him not, for we will grow
Ready like the field we mow:
Like the bending barley lithe,   40
Ready for Time's whetted scythe.
   Rink-a-tink, rink-a-tink, rink-a-tink-a-tink!

1847

ELIZABETH BARRETT BROWNING

Sonnets from the Portuguese*

I

I thought once how Theocritus* had sung
Of the sweet years, the dear and wished-for years,
Who each one in a gracious hand appears
To bear a gift for mortals, old or young:
And, as I mused it in his antique tongue,
I saw, in gradual vision through my tears,
The sweet, sad years, the melancholy years,
Those of my own life, who by turns had flung
A shadow across me. Straightway I was 'ware,
So weeping, how a mystic Shape did move   10
Behind me, and drew me backward by the hair,
And a voice said in mastery while I strove, . . .
'Guess now who holds thee!'—'Death,' I said. But, there,
The silver answer rang, . . . 'Not Death, but Love.'

3

Unlike are we, unlike, O princely Heart!
Unlike our uses and our destinies.
Our ministering two angels look surprise
On one another, as they strike athwart
Their wings in passing. Thou, bethink thee, art
A guest for queens to social pageantries,
With gages from a hundred brighter eyes
Than tears even can make mine, to play thy part
Of chief musician. What hast *thou* to do
With looking from the lattice-lights at me,   10
A poor, tired, wandering singer, singing through
The dark, and leaning up a cypress tree?
The chrism is on thine head,—on mine, the dew,—
And Death must dig the level where these agree.

4

Thou hast thy calling to some palace-floor,
Most gracious singer of high poems! where
The dancers will break footing, from the care
Of watching up thy pregnant lips for more.
And dost thou lift this house's latch too poor
For hand of thine? and canst thou think and bear
To let thy music drop here unaware
In folds of golden fullness at my door?
Look up and see the casement broken in,
The bats and owlets builders in the roof!　　　　　10
My cricket chirps against thy mandolin.
Hush, call no echo up in further proof
Of desolation! there's a voice within
That weeps . . . as thou must sing . . . alone, aloof.

5

I lift my heavy heart up solemnly,
As once Electra* her sepulchral urn,
And, looking in thine eyes, I overturn
The ashes at thy feet. Behold and see
What a great heap of grief lay hid in me,
And how the red wild sparkles dimly burn
Through the ashen greyness. If thy foot in scorn
Could tread them out to darkness utterly,
It might be well perhaps. But if instead
Thou wait beside me for the wind to blow　　　　　10
The grey dust up, . . . those laurels on thine head,
O my Beloved, will not shield thee so,
That none of all the fires shall scorch and shred
The hair beneath. Stand farther off then! go.

14

If thou must love me, let it be for nought
Except for love's sake only. Do not say
'I love her for her smile . . . her look . . . her way
Of speaking gently, . . . for a trick of thought
That falls in well with mine, and certes brought
A sense of pleasant ease on such a day'—
For these things in themselves, Beloved, may

Be changed, or change for thee,—and love, so wrought,
May be unwrought so. Neither love me for
Thine own dear pity's wiping my cheeks dry,—   10
A creature might forget to weep, who bore
Thy comfort long, and lose thy love thereby!
But love me for love's sake, that evermore
Thou mayst love on, through love's eternity.

19

The soul's Rialto* hath its merchandise
I barter curl for curl upon that mart,
And from my poet's forehead to my heart,
Receive this lock which outweighs argosies,—
As purply black, as erst, to Pindar's* eyes,
The dim purpureal tresses gloomed athwart
The nine white Muse-brows. For this counterpart, . . .
Thy bay-crown's shade, Beloved, I surmise,
Still lingers on thy curl, it is so black!
Thus, with a fillet of smooth kissing breath,   10
I tie the shadow safe from gliding back,
And lay the gift where nothing hindereth,
Here on my heart, as on thy brow, to lack
No natural heart till mine grows cold in death.

24

Let the world's sharpness like a clasping knife
Shut in upon itself and do no harm
In this close hand of Love, now soft and warm,
And let us hear no sound of human strife
After the click of the shutting. Life to life—
I lean upon thee, dear, without alarm,
And feel as safe as guarded by a charm
Against the stab of worldlings, who if rife
Are weak to injure. Very whitely still
The lilies of our lives may reassure   10
Their blossoms from their roots, accessible
Alone to heavenly dews that drop not fewer:
Growing straight, out of man's reach, on the hill.
God only, who made us rich, can make us poor.

43

How do I love thee? Let me count the ways.
I love thee to the depth and breadth and height
My soul can reach, when feeling out of sight
For the ends of Being and ideal Grace.
I love thee to the level of every day's
Most quiet need, by sun and candlelight.
I love thee freely, as men strive for Right;
I love thee purely, as they turn from Praise.
I love thee with the passion put to use
In my old griefs, and with my childhood's faith.   10
I love thee with a love I seemed to lose
With my lost saints,—I love thee with the breath,
Smiles, tears of all my life!—and, if God choose,
I shall but love thee better after death.

1847

Aurora Leigh*
Book I

Of writing many books there is no end;
And I who have written much in prose and verse
For others' uses, will write now for mine,—
Will write my story for my better self,
As when you paint your portrait for a friend,
Who keeps it in a drawer and looks at it
Long after he has ceased to love you, just
To hold together what he was and is.
I, writing thus, am still what men call young;
I have not so far left the coasts of life   10
To travel inland, that I cannot hear
That murmur of the outer Infinite
Which unweaned babies smile at in their sleep
When wondered at for smiling; not so far.
But still I catch my mother at her post
Beside the nursery door, with finger up,
'Hush, hush—here's too much noise!' while her sweet eyes
Leap forward, taking part against her word,

In the child's riot. Still I sit and feel
My father's slow hand, when she had left us both,   20
Stroke out my childish curls across his knee,
And hear Assunta's daily jest (she knew
He liked it better than a better jest)
Inquire how many golden scudi went
To make such ringlets. O my father's hand,
Stroke heavily, heavily the poor hair down,
Draw, press the child's head closer to thy knee!
I'm still too young, too young, to sit alone.

I write. My mother was a Florentine,
Whose rare blue eyes were shut from seeing me   30
When scarcely I was four years old, my life
A poor spark snatched up from a failing lamp
Which went out therefore. She was weak and frail;
She could not bear the joy of giving life,
The mother's rapture slew her. If her kiss
Had left a longer weight upon my lips
It might have steadied the uneasy breath,
And reconciled and fraternised my soul
With the new order. As it was, indeed,
I felt a mother-want about the world,   40
And still went seeking, like a bleating lamb
Left out at night in shutting up the fold—
As restless as a nest-deserted bird
Grown chill through something being away, though what
It knows not. I, Aurora Leigh, was born
To make my father sadder, and myself
Not overjoyous, truly. Women know
The way to rear up children (to be just),
They know a simple, merry, tender knack
Of tying sashes, fitting baby-shoes,   50
And stringing pretty words that make no sense,
And kissing full sense into empty words,
Which things are corals to cut life upon,
Although such trifles: children learn by such,
Love's holy earnest in a pretty play
And get not over-early solemnised,
But seeing, as in a rose-bush, Love's Divine
Which burns and hurts not,*—not a single bloom,—

Become aware and unafraid of Love.
Such good do mothers. Fathers love as well   60
—Mine did, I know,—but still with heavier brains,
And wills more consciously responsible,
And not as wisely, since less foolishly;
So mothers have God's licence to be missed.

My father was an austere Englishman,
Who, after a dry lifetime spent at home
In college-learning, law, and parish talk,
Was flooded with a passion unaware,
His whole provisioned and complacent past
Drowned out from him that moment. As he stood   70
In Florence, where he had come to spend a month
And note the secret of Da Vinci's drains,
He musing somewhat absently perhaps
Some English question . . . whether men should pay
The unpopular but necessary tax
With left or right hand—in the alien sun
In that great square of Santissima
There drifted past him (scarcely marked enough
To move his comfortable island scorn)
A train of priestly banners, cross and psalm,   80
The white-veiled rose-crowned maidens holding up
Tall tapers, weighty for such wrists, aslant
To the blue luminous tremor of the air,
And letting drop the white wax as they went
To eat the bishop's wafer at the church;
From which long trail of chanting priests and girls,
A face flashed like a cymbal on his face
And shook with silent clangour brain and heart,
Transfiguring him to music. Thus, even thus,
He too received his sacramental gift   90
With eucharistic meanings; for he loved.
And thus beloved, she died. I've heard it said
That but to see him in the first surprise
Of widower and father, nursing me,
Unmothered little child of four years old,
His large man's hands afraid to touch my curls,
As if the gold would tarnish,—his grave lips
Contriving such a miserable smile

As if he knew needs must, or I should die,
And yet 'twas hard,—would almost make the stones   100
Cry out for pity. There's a verse he set
In Santa Croce to her memory,—
'Weep for an infant too young to weep much
When death removed this mother!'—stops the mirth
Today on women's faces when they walk
With rosy children hanging on their gowns,
Under the cloister to escape the sun
That scorches in the piazza. After which
He left our Florence and made haste to hide
Himself, his prattling child, and silent grief,   110
Among the mountains above Pelago;
Because unmothered babes, he thought, had need
Of mother nature more than others use,
And Pan's white goats, with udders warm and full
Of mystic contemplations, come to feed
Poor milkless lips of orphans like his own—
Such scholar-scraps he talked, I've heard from friends,
For even prosaic men who wear grief long
Will get to wear it as a hat aside
With a flower stuck in't. Father, then, and child,   120
We lived among the mountains many years,
God's silence on the outside of the house,
And we who did not speak too loud within,
And old Assunta to make up the fire,
Crossing herself whene'er a sudden flame
Which lightened from the firewood, made alive
That picture of my mother on the wall.

The painter drew it after she was dead,
And when the face was finished, throat and hands,
Her cameriera carried him, in hate   130
Of the English-fashioned shroud, the last brocade
She dressed in at the Pitti; 'he should paint
No sadder thing than that,' she swore, 'to wrong
Her poor signora.' Therefore very strange
The effect was. I, a little child, would crouch
For hours upon the floor with knees drawn up,
And gaze across them, half in terror, half
In adoration, at the picture there,—

That swan-like supernatural white life
Just sailing upward from the red stiff silk   140
Which seemed to have no part in it nor power
To keep it from quite breaking out of bounds.
For hours I sat and stared. Assunta's awe
And my poor father's melancholy eyes
Still pointed that way. That way went my thoughts
When wandering beyond sight. And as I grew
In years, I mixed, confused, unconsciously,
Whatever I last read or heard or dreamed,
Abhorrent, admirable, beautiful,
Pathetical, or ghastly, or grotesque,   150
With still that face . . . which did not therefore change,
But kept the mystic level of all forms,
Hates, fears, and admirations, was by turns
Ghost, fiend, and angel, fairy, witch, and sprite,
A dauntless Muse who eyes a dreadful Fate,
A loving Psyche* who loses sight of Love,
A still Medusa* with mild milky brows
All curdled and all clothed upon with snakes
Whose slime falls fast as sweat will; or anon
Our Lady of the Passion*, stabbed with swords   160
Where the Babe sucked; or Lamia* in her first
Moonlighted pallor, ere she shrunk and blinked
And shuddering wriggled down to the unclean;
Or my own mother, leaving her last smile
In her last kiss upon the baby-mouth
My father pushed down on the bed for that,—
Or my dead mother, without smile or kiss,
Buried at Florence. All which images,
Concentrated on the picture, glassed themselves
Before my meditative childhood, as   170
The incoherencies of change and death
Are represented fully, mixed and merged,
In the smooth fair mystery of perpetual Life.
And while I stared away my childish wits
Upon my mother's picture (ah, poor child!),
My father, who through love had suddenly
Thrown off the old conventions, broken loose
From chin-bands of the soul like Lazarus,
Yet had no time to learn to talk and walk

Or grow anew familiar with the sun,—   180
Who had reached to freedom, not to action, lived,
But lived as one entranced, with thoughts, not aims,—
Whom love had unmade from a common man
But not completed to an uncommon man,—
My father taught me what he had learnt the best
Before he died and left me,—grief and love.
And, seeing we had books among the hills,
Strong words of counselling souls confederate
With vocal pines and waters,—out of books
He taught me all the ignorance of men,   190
And how God laughs in heaven when any man
Says, 'Here I'm learned; this, I understand;
In that, I am never caught at fault or doubt.'
He sent the schools to school, demonstrating
A fool will pass for such through one mistake,
While a philosopher will pass for such,
Through said mistakes being ventured in the gross
And heaped up to a system.
                          I am like,
They tell me, my dear father. Broader brows
Howbeit, upon a slenderer undergrowth   200
Of delicate features,—paler, near as grave;
But then my mother's smile breaks up the whole,
And makes it better sometimes than itself.
So, nine full years, our days were hid with God
Among his mountains: I was just thirteen,
Still growing like the plants from unseen roots
In tongue-tied Springs,—and suddenly awoke
To full life and life's needs and agonies
With an intense, strong, struggling heart beside   210
A stone-dead father. Life, struck sharp on death,
Makes awful lightning. His last word was 'Love—'
'Love, my child, love, love!'—(then he had done with grief)
'Love, my child.' Ere I answered he was gone,
And none was left to love in all the world.

There, ended childhood. What succeeded next
I recollect as, after fevers, men
Thread back the passage of delirium,
Missing the turn still, baffled by the door;

Smooth endless days, notched here and there with knives, 220
A weary, wormy darkness, spurred i' the flank
With flame, that it should eat and end itself
Like some tormented scorpion. Then at last
I do remember clearly how there came
A stranger with authority, not right
(I thought not), who commanded, caught me up
From old Assunta's neck; how, with a shriek,
She let me go,—while I, with ears too full
Of my father's silence to shriek back a word,
In all a child's astonishment at grief   230
Stared at the wharf-edge where she stood and moaned,
My poor Assunta, where she stood and moaned!
The white walls, the blue hills, my Italy,
Drawn backward from the shuddering steamer-deck
Like one in anger drawing back her skirts
Which suppliants catch at. Then the bitter sea
Inexorably pushed between us both
And, sweeping up the ship with my despair,
Threw us out as a pasture to the stars.

Ten nights and days we voyaged on the deep;   240
Ten nights and days without the common face
Of any day or night; the moon and sun
Cut off from the green reconciling earth,
To starve into a blind ferocity
And glare unnatural; the very sky
(Dropping its bell-net down upon the sea,
As if no human heart should 'scape alive)
Bedraggled with the desolating salt,
Until it seemed no more that holy heaven
To which my father went. All new and strange;   250
The universe turned stranger, for a child.

Then, land!—then, England! oh, the frosty cliffs
Looked cold upon me. Could I find a home
Among those mean red houses through the fog?
And when I heard my father's language first
From alien lips which had no kiss for mine
I wept aloud, then laughed, then wept, then wept,
And someone near me said the child was mad

Through much sea-sickness. The train swept us on:
Was this my father's England? the great isle?   260
The ground seemed cut up from the fellowship
Of verdure, field from field, as man from man;
The skies themselves looked low and positive,
As almost you could touch them with a hand,
And dared to do it they were so far off
From God's celestial crystals; all things blurred
And dull and vague. Did Shakespeare and his mates
Absorb the light here?—not a hill or stone
With heart to strike a radiant colour up
Or active outline on the indifferent air.   270

I think I see my father's sister stand
Upon the hall-step of her country-house
To give me welcome. She stood straight and calm,
Her somewhat narrow forehead braided tight
As if for taming accidental thoughts
From possible pulses; brown hair pricked with gray
By frigid use of life (she was not old,
Although my father's elder by a year),
A nose drawn sharply, yet in delicate lines;
A close mild mouth, a little soured about   280
The ends, through speaking unrequited loves
Or peradventure niggardly half-truths;
Eyes of no colour,—once they might have smiled,
But never, never have forgot themselves
In smiling; cheeks, in which was yet a rose
Of perished summers, like a rose in a book,
Kept more for ruth than pleasure,—if past bloom,
Past fading also.
                         She had lived, we'll say,
A harmless life, she called a virtuous life,
A quiet life, which was not life at all   290
(But that, she had not lived enough to know),
Between the vicar and the county squires,
The lord-lieutenant looking down sometimes
From the empyrean to assure their souls
Against chance vulgarisms, and, in the abyss,
The apothecary, looked on once a year
To prove their soundness of humility.

The poor-club exercised her Christian gifts
Of kniting stockings, stitching petticoats,
Because we are of one flesh, afterall,
And need one flannel (with a proper sense)
Of difference in the quality)—and still
The book-club, guarded from your modern trick
Of shaking dangerous questions from the crease,
Preserved her intellectual. She had lived   300
A sort of cage-bird life, born in a cage,
Accounting that to leap from perch to perch
Was act and joy enough for any bird.
Dear heaven, how silly are the things that live
In thickets, and eat berries!
                              I alas,
A wild bird scarcely fledged, was brought to her cage,
And she was there to meet me. Very kind.
Bring the clean water, give out the fresh seed.

She stood upon the steps to welcome me,
Calm, in black garb. I clung about her neck,—   310
Young babes, who catch at every shred of wool
To draw the new light closer, catch and cling
Less blindly. In my ears my father's word
Hummed ignorantly, as the sea in shells,
'Love, love, my child.' She, black there with my grief,
Might feel my love—she was his sister once—
I clung to her. A moment she seemed moved,
Kissed me with cold lips, suffered me to cling,
And drew me feebly through the hall into
The room she sat in.
                              There, with some strange spasm   320
Of pain and passion, she wrung loose my hands
Imperiously, and held me at arm's length,
And with two grey-steel naked-bladed eyes
Searched through my face,—ay, stabbed it through and
          through,
Through brows and cheeks and chin, as if to find
A wicked murderer in my innocent face,
If not here, there perhaps. Then, drawing breath,
She struggled for her ordinary calm—
And missed it rather,—told me not to shrink,

As if she had told me not to lie or swear,—   330
'She loved my father and would love me too
As long as I deserved it.' Very kind.

I understood her meaning afterward;
She thought to find my mother in my face,
And questioned it for that. For she, my aunt,
Had loved my father truly, as she could,
And hated, with the gall of gentle souls,
My Tuscan mother who had fooled away
A wise man from wise courses, a good man
From obvious duties, and, depriving her,   340
His sister, of the household precedence,
Had wronged his tenants, robbed his native land,
And made him mad, alike by life and death,
In love and sorrow. She had pored for years
What sort of woman could be suitable
To her sort of hate, to entertain it with,
And so, her very curiosity
Became hate too, and all the idealism
She ever used in life was used for hate,
Till hate, so nourished, did exceed at last   350
The love from which it grew, in strength and heat,
And wrinkled her smooth conscience with a sense
Of disputable virtue (say not, sin)
When Christian doctrine was enforced at church.

And thus my father's sister was to me
My mother's hater. From that day she did
Her duty to me (I appreciate it
In her own word as spoken to herself),
Her duty, in large measure, well pressed out,
But measured always. She was generous, bland,   360
More courteous than was tender, gave me still
The first place,—as if fearful that God's saints
Would look down suddenly and say, 'Herein
You missed a point, I think, through lack of love.'
Alas, a mother never is afraid
Of speaking angerly to any child,
Since love, she knows, is justified of love.

And I, I was a good child on the whole,
A meek and manageable child. Why not?
I did not live, to have the faults of life: 370
There seemed more true life in my father's grave
Than in all England. Since *that* threw me off
Who fain would cleave (his latest will, they say,
Consigned me to his land), I only thought
Of lying quiet there where I was thrown
Like sea-weed on the rocks, and suffering her
To prick me to a pattern with her pin,
Fibre from fibre, delicate leaf from leaf,
And dry out from my drowned anatomy
The last sea-salt left in me.
                         So it was.   380
I broke the copious curls upon my head
In braids, because she liked smooth-ordered hair.
I left off saying my sweet Tuscan words
Which still at any stirring of the heart
Came up to float across the English phrase
As lilies (*Bene* or *Che che*), because
She liked my father's child to speak his tongue.
I learnt the collects and the catechism,
The creeds, from Athanasius back to Nice,
The Articles, the Tracts *against* the times*   390
(By no means Buonaventure's 'Prick of Love*),
And various popular synopses of
Inhuman doctrines never taught by John,
Because she liked instructed piety.
I learnt my complement of classic French
(Kept pure of Balzac and neologism)
And German also, since she liked a range
Of liberal education,—tongues, not books.
I learnt a little algebra, a little
Of the mathematics,—brushed with extreme flounce   400
The circle of sciences, because
She misliked women who are frivolous.
I learnt the royal genealogies
Of Oviedo, the internal laws
Of the Burmese empire,—by how many feet
Mount Chimborazo outsoars Teneriffe,
What navigable river joins itself

To Lara, and what census of the year five
Was taken at Klagenfurt,—because she liked
A general insight into useful facts,   410
I learnt much music,—such as would have been
As quite impossible in Johnson's day
As still it might be wished—fine sleights of hand
And unimagined fingering, shuffling off
The hearer's soul through hurricanes of notes
To a noisy Tophet; and I drew . . . costumes
From French engravings, nereids neatly draped
(With smirks of simmering godship): I washed in
Landscapes from nature (rather say, washed out).
I danced the polka and Cellarius,   420
Spun glass, stuffed birds, and modelled flowers in wax,
Because she liked accomplishments in girls.
I read a score of books on womanhood
To prove, if women do not think at all,
They may teach thinking (to a maiden aunt
Or else the author),—books that boldly assert
Their right of comprehending husband's talk
When not too deep, and even of answering
With pretty 'may it please you', or 'so it is',—
Their rapid insight and fine aptitude,   430
Particular worth and general missionariness,
As long as they keep quiet by the fire
And never say 'no' when the world says 'ay',
For that is fatal,—their angelic reach
Of virtue, chiefly used to sit and darn,
And fatten household sinners,—their, in brief,
Potential faculty in everything
Of abdicating power in it: she owned
She liked a woman to be womanly,
And, English women, she thanked God and sighed   440
(Some people always sigh in thanking God),
Were models to the universe. And last
I learnt cross-stitch, because she did not like
To see me wear the night with empty hands
A-doing nothing. So, my shepherdess
Was something after all (the pastoral saints
Be praised for't), leaning lovelorn with pink eyes
To match her shoes, when I mistook the silks;

Her head uncrushed by that round weight of hat
So strangely similar to the tortoise-shell   450
Which slew the tragic poet.

                              By the way,
The works of women are symbolical.
We sew, sew, prick our fingers, dull our sight,
Producing what? A pair of slippers, sir,
To put on when you're weary—or a stool
To stumble over and vex you . . . 'curse that stool!'
Or else at best, a cushion, where you lean
And sleep, and dream of something we are not
But would be for your sake. Alas, alas!
This hurts most, this—that after all we are paid   460
The worth of our work, perhaps.

                              In looking down
Those years of education (to return)
I wondered if Brinvilliers* suffered more
In the water-torture . . . flood succeeding flood
To drench the incapable throat and split the veins . . .
Than I did. Certain of your feebler souls
Go out in such a process; many pine
To a sick inodorous light; my own endured:
I had relations in the Unseen, and drew
The elemental nutriment and heat   470
From nature, as earth feels the sun at nights,
Or as a babe sucks surely in the dark.
I kept the life thrust on me, on the outside
Of the inner life with all its ample room
For heart and lungs, for will and intellect,
Inviolable by conventions . . .

My books! At last because the time was ripe,
I chanced upon the poets.

                              As the earth
Plunges in fury, when the internal fires
Have reached and pricked her heart, and throwing flat   480
The marts and temples, the triumphal gates
And towers of observation, clears herself
To elemental freedom—thus, my soul,
At poetry's divine first finger-touch,
Let go conventions and sprang up surprised,

Convicted of the great eternities
Before two worlds.
                What's this, Aurora Leigh,
You write so of the poets, and not laugh?
Those virtuous liars, dreamers after dark,
Exaggerators of the sun and moon,   490
And soothsayers in a tea-cup?
                      I write so
Of the only truth-tellers now left to God,
The only speakers of essential truth,
Opposed to relative, comparative,
And temporal truths; the only holders by
His sun-skirts, through conventional gray glooms;
The only teachers who instruct mankind
From just a shadow on a charnel-wall
To find man's veritable stature out
Erect, sublime,—the measure of a man,   500
And that's the measure of an angel, says
The apostle. Ay, and while your common men
Lay telegraphs, gauge railroads, reign, reap, dine,
And dust the flaunty carpets of the world
For kings to walk on, or our president,
The poet suddenly will catch them up
With his voice like a thunder,—'This is soul,
This is life, this word is being said in heaven,
Here's God down on us! What are you about?'
How all those workers start amid their work,   510
Look round, look up, and feel a moment's space,
That carpet-dusting, though a pretty trade,
Is not the imperative labour after all.

My own best poets, am I one with you,
That thus I love you,—or but one through love?
Does all this smell of thyme about my feet
Conclude my visit to your holy hill
In personal presence, or but testify
The rustling of your vesture through my dreams
With influent odours? Why my joy and pain,   520
My thought and aspiration, like the stops
Of pipe or flute, are absolutely dumb
Unless melodious, do you play on me

My pipers,—and if, sooth, you did not blow,
Would no sound come? or is the music mine,
As a man's voice or breath is called his own,
Inbreathed by the Life-breather? There's a doubt
For cloudy seasons!
                           But the sun was high
When first I felt my pulses set themselves
For concord; when the rhythmic turbulence   530
Of blood and brain swept outward upon words,
As wind upon the alders, blanching them
By turning up their under-natures till
They trembled in dilation. O delight
And triumph of the poet, who would say
A man's mere 'yes', a woman's common 'no',
A little human hope of that or this,
And says the word so that it burns you through
With a special revelation, shakes the heart
Of all the men and women in the world,   540
As if one came back from the dead and spoke,
With eyes too happy, a familiar thing
Become divine i' the utterance! while for him
The poet, speaker, he expands with joy;
The palpitating angel in his flesh
Thrills inly with consenting fellowship
To those innumerous spirits who sun themselves
Outside of time.
                    O life, O poetry,
—Which means life in life! cognisant of life
Beyond this blood-beat, passionate for truth   550
Beyond these senses!—poetry, my life,
My eagle, with both grappling feet still hot
From Zeus' thunder, who hast ravished me
Away from all the shepherds, sheep, and dogs,
And set me in the Olympian roar and round
Of luminous faces for a cup-bearer,
To keep the mouths of all the godheads moist
For everlasting laughters,—I myself
Half drunk across the beaker with their eyes!
How those gods look!
                         Enough so, Ganymede,*   560
We shall not bear above a round or two.

We drop the golden cup at Hebe's foot
And swoon back to the earth,—and find ourselves
Face-down among the pine-cones, cold with dew,
While the dogs bark, and many a shepherd scoffs,
'What's come now to the youth?' Ups and downs
Have poets.
        Am I such indeed? The name
Is royal, and to sign it like a queen
Is what I dare not,—though some royal blood
Would seem to tingle in me now and then,   570
With sense of power and ache,—with imposthumes
And manias usual to the race. Howbeit
I dare not; 'tis too easy to go mad
And ape a Bourbon in a crown of straws;
The thing's too common.
        Many fervent souls
Strike rhyme on rhyme, who would strike steel on steel
If steel had offered, in a restless heat
Of doing something. Many tender souls
Have strung their losses on a rhyming thread,
As children cowslips;—the more pains they take,   580
The work more withers. Young men, ay, and maids,
Too often sow their wild oats in tame verse,
Before they sit down under their own vine
And live for use. Alas, near all the birds
Will sing at dawn,—and yet we do not take
The chaffering swallow for the holy lark.
In those days, though, I never analysed,
Not even myself. Analysis comes late.
You catch a sight of Nature, earliest,
In full front sun-face, and your eyelids wink   590
And drop before the wonder of 't; you miss
The form, through seeing the light. I lived, those days,
And wrote because I lived—unlicensed else;
My heart beat in my brain. Life's violent flood
Abolished bounds,—and, which my neighbour's field,
Which mine, what mattered? It is thus in youth!
We play at leap-frog over the god Term;
The love within us and the love without
Are mixed, confounded; if we are loved or love
We scarce distinguish: thus, with other power;   600

Being acted on and acting seem the same:
In that first onrush of life's chariot-wheels,
We know not if the forests move or we.

And so, like most young poets, in a flush
Of individual life I poured myself
Along the veins of others, and achieved
Mere lifeless imitations of live verse,
And made the living answer for the dead,
Profaning nature. 'Touch not, do not taste,
Nor handle,'—we're too legal, who write young: 610
We beat the phorminx till we hurt our thumbs,
As if still ignorant of counterpoint;
We call the Muse,—'O Muse, benignant Muse,'—
As if we had seen her purple-braided head,
With the eyes in it, start between the boughs
As often as a stag's. What make-believe,
With so much earnest! what effete results
From virile efforts! what cold wire-drawn odes
From such white heats!—bucolics, where the cows
Would scare the writer if they splashed the mud   620
In lashing off the flies,—didactics, driven
Against the heels of what the master said;
And counterfeiting epics, shrill with trumps
A babe might blow between two straining cheeks
Of bubbled rose, to make his mother laugh;
And elegiac griefs, and songs of love,
Like cast-off nosegays picked up on the road,
The worse for being warm: all these things, writ
On happy mornings, with a morning heart,
That leaps for love, is active for resolve,   630
Weak for art only. Oft, the ancient forms
Will thrill, indeed, in carrying the young blood,
The wine-skins, now and then, a little warped,
Will crack even, as the new wine gurgles in.
Spare the old bottles!—spill not the new wine.

By Keats's soul, the man who never stepped
In gradual progress like another man,
But, turning grandly on his central self,
Ensphered himself in twenty perfect years

And died, not young (the life of a long life   640
Distilled to a mere drop, falling like a tear
Upon the world's cold cheek to make it burn
For ever); by that strong excepted soul,
I count it strange and hard to understand
That nearly all young poets should write old,
That Pope was sexagenary at sixteen,
And beardless Byron academical,
And so with others. It may be perhaps
Such have not settled long and deep enough
In trance, to attain to clairvoyance,—and still   650
The memory mixes with the vision, spoils,
And works it turbid.

              Or perhaps, again,
In order to discover the Muse-Sphinx,*
The melancholy desert must sweep round,
Behind you as before.—

              For me, I wrote
False poems, like the rest, and thought them true
Because myself was true in writing them.
I peradventure have writ true ones since
With less complacence.

              But I could not hide
My quickening inner life from those at watch.   660
They saw a light at a window, now and then,
They had not set there: who had set it there?
My father's sister started when she caught
My soul agaze in my eyes. She could not say
I had no business with a sort of soul,
But plainly she objected,—and demurred
That souls were dangerous things to carry straight
Through all the spilt saltpetre of the world.
She said sometimes, 'Aurora, have you done
Your task this morning? have you read that book?   670
And are you ready for the crochet here?'—
As if she said, 'I know there's something wrong;
I know I have not ground you down enough
To flatten and bake you to a wholesome crust
For household uses and proprieties,
Before the rain has got into my barn
And set the grains a-sprouting. What, you're green

With out-door impudence? You almost grow?'
To which I answered, 'Would she hear my task,
And verify my abstract of the book?   680
Or should I sit down to the crochet work?
Was such her pleasure?' Then I sat and teased
The patient needle till it split the thread,
Which oozed off from it in meandering lace
From hour to hour. I was not, therefore, sad;
My soul was singing at a work apart
Behind the wall of sense, as safe from harm
As sings the lark when sucked up out of sight
In vortices of glory and blue air.

And so, through forced work and spontaneous work,   690
The inner life informed the outer life,
Reduced the irregular blood to a settled rhythm,
Made cool the forehead with fresh-sprinkling dreams,
And, rounding to the spheric soul the thin,
Pined body, struck a colour up the cheeks
Though somewhat faint . . .

                                                        1856

CHRISTINA ROSSETTI

Song

When I am dead, my dearest,
  Sing no sad songs for me;
Plant thou no roses at my head,
  Nor shady cypress tree;
Be the green grass above me
  With showers and dewdrops wet;
And if thou wilt, remember,
  And if thou wilt, forget.

I shall not see the shadows,
  I shall not feel the rain;   10
I shall not hear the nightingale
  Sing on, as if in pain:
And dreaming through the twilight
  That doth not rise nor set,
Haply I may remember,
  And haply may forget.

                                        1848

Song

Oh roses for the flush of youth,
  And laurel for the perfect prime;
But pluck an ivy branch for me
  Grown old before my time.

Oh violets for the grave of youth,
  And bay for those dead in their prime;
Give me the withered leaves I chose
  Before in the old time.

                                        1849

Remember

Remember me when I am gone away,
  Gone far away into the silent land;
  When you can no more hold me by the hand,
Nor I half turn to go yet turning stay.
Remember me when no more day by day
  You tell me of our future that you planned:
  Only remember me; you understand
It will be late to counsel then or pray.
Yet if you should forget me for a while   10
  And afterwards remember, do not grieve:
  For if the darkness and corruption leave
  A vestige of the thoughts that once I had,
Better by far you should forget and smile
  Than that you should remember and be sad.

1849

The Bourne

Underneath the growing grass,
  Underneath the living flowers,
  Deeper than the sound of showers:
  There we shall not count the hours
By the shadows as they pass.

Youth and health will be but vain,
  Beauty reckoned of no worth:
  There a very little girth
  Can hold round what once the earth
Seemed too narrow to contain.

1854

A Triad

Three sang of love together: one with lips
  Crimson, with cheeks and bosom in a glow,
Flushed to the yellow hair and finger tips;
  And one there sang who soft and smooth as snow
  Bloomed like a tinted hyacinth at a show;
And one was blue with famine after love,
  Who like a harpstring snapped rang harsh and low
The burden of what those were singing of.
One shamed herself in love; one temperately
  Grew gross in soulless love, a sluggish wife;   10
One famished died for love. Thus two of three
  Took death for love and won him after strife;
One droned in sweetness like a fattened bee:
  All on the threshold, yet all short of life.

              1856

A Birthday

My heart is like a singing bird
  Whose nest is in a watered shoot;
My heart is like an apple tree
  Whose boughs are bent with thickset fruit;
My heart is like a rainbow shell
  That paddles in a halcyon sea;
My heart is gladder than all these
  Because my love is come to me.

Raise me a dais of silk and down;
  Hang it with vair and purple dyes;   10
Carve it in doves and pomegranates,
  And peacocks with a hundred eyes;
Work it in gold and silver grapes,
  In leaves and silver fleurs-de-lys;
Because the birthday of my life
  Is come, my love is come to me.

             1857

Winter: My Secret

I tell my secret? No indeed, not I:
Perhaps some day, who knows?
But not today; it froze, and blows, and snows,
And you're too curious: fie!
You want to hear it? well:
Only, my secret's mine, and I won't tell.

Or, after all, perhaps there's none:
Suppose there is no secret after all,
But only just my fun.
Today's a nipping day, a biting day;   10
In which one wants a shawl,
A veil, a cloak, and other wraps:
I cannot open to everyone who taps,
And let the draught come whistling thro' my hall;
Come bounding and surrounding me,
Come buffeting, astounding me,
Nipping and clipping thro' my wraps and all.
I wear my mask for warmth: who ever shows
His nose to Russian snows
To be pecked at by every wind that blows?   20
You would not peck? I thank you for good will,
Believe, but leave that truth untested still.

Spring's an expansive time: yet I don't trust
March with its peck of dust,
Nor April with its rainbow-crowned brief showers,
Nor even May, whose flowers
One frost may wither thro' the sunless hours.

Perhaps some languid summer day,
When drowsy birds sing less and less,
And golden fruit is ripening to excess,   30
If there's not too much sun nor too much cloud,
And the warm wind is neither still nor loud,
Perhaps my secret I may say,
Or you may guess.

1857

Goblin Market

Morning and evening
Maids heard the goblins cry:
'Come buy our orchard fruits,
Come buy, come buy:
Apples and quinces,
Lemons and oranges,
Plump unpecked cherries,
Melons and raspberries,
Bloom-down-cheeked peaches,   10
Swart-headed mulberries,
Wild free-born cranberries,
Crab-apples, dewberries,
Pine-apples, blackberries,
Apricots, strawberries;
All ripe together
In summer weather,
Morns that pass by,
Fair eves that fly;
Come buy, come buy:
Our grapes fresh from the vine,   20
Pomegranates full and fine,
Dates and sharp bullaces,
Rare pears and greengages,
Damsons and bilberries,
Taste them and try:
Currants and gooseberries,
Bright-fire-like barberries,
Figs to fill your mouth,
Citrons from the South,
Sweet to tongue and sound to eye;   30
Come buy, come buy.'

Evening by evening
Among the brookside rushes,
Laura bowed her head to hear,
Lizzie veiled her blushes:
Crouching close together,
In the cooling weather,

With clasping arms and cautioning lips,
With tingling cheeks and finger tips.
'Lie close,' Laura said,   40
Pricking up her golden head:
'We must not look at goblin men,
We must not buy their fruits:
Who knows upon what soil they fed
Their hungry thirsty roots?'
'Come buy,' called the goblins
Hobbling down the glen.
'Oh,' cried Lizzie, 'Laura, Laura,
You should not peep at goblin men.'
Lizzie covered up her eyes,   50
Covered close lest they should look;
Laura reared her glossy head,
And whispered like the restless brook:
'Look, Lizzie, look, Lizzie,
Down the glen tramp little men.
One hauls a basket,
One bears a plate,
One hugs a golden dish
Of many pounds weight.
How fair the vine must grow   60
Whose grapes are so luscious;
How warm the wind must blow
Thro' those fruit bushes.'
'No,' said Lizzie: 'No, no, no;
Their offers should not charm us,
Their evil gifts would harm us.'
She thrust a dimpled finger
In each ear, shut eyes and ran:
Curious Laura chose to linger
Wondering at each merchant man.   70
One had a cat's face,
One whisked a tail,
One tramped at a rat's pace,
One crawled like a snail,
One like a wombat prowled obtuse and furry,
One like a ratel tumbled hurry skurry.
She heard a voice like voice of doves
Cooing all together:

They sounded kind and full of loves
In the pleasant weather. 80

Laura stretched her gleaming neck
Like a rush-imbedded swan,
Like a lily from the beck,
Like a moonlit poplar branch,
Like a vessel at the launch
When its last restraint is gone.

Backwards up the mossy glen
Turned and trooped the goblin men,
With their shrill repeated cry,
'Come buy, come buy.' 90
When they reached where Laura was
They stood stock still upon the moss,
Leering at each other,
Brother with queer brother.
Signalling each other,
Brother with sly brother.
One set his basket down,
One reared his plate;
One began to weave a crown
Of tendrils, leaves and rough nuts brown 100
(Men sell not such in any town);
One heaved the golden weight
Of dish and fruit to offer her;
'Come buy, come buy,' was still their cry.
Laura stared but did not stir,
Longed but had no money:
The whisk-tailed merchant bade her taste
In tones as smooth as honey,
The cat-faced purred,
The rat-paced spoke a word 110
Of welcome, and the snail-paced even was heard;
One parrot-voiced and jolly
Cried 'Pretty Goblin' still for 'Pretty Polly';
One whistled like a bird.

But sweet-tooth Laura spoke in haste:
'Good folk, I have no coin;

To take were to purloin:
I have no copper in my purse,
I have no silver either,
And all my gold is on the furze   120
That shakes in windy weather
Above the rusty heather.'
'You have much gold upon your head,'
They answered all together:
'Buy from us with a golden curl.'
She clipped a precious golden lock,
She dropped a tear more rare than pearl,
Then sucked their fruit globes fair or red:
Sweeter than honey from the rock,
Stronger than man-rejoicing wine,   130
Clearer than water flowed that juice;
She never tasted such before,
How should it cloy with length of use?
She sucked and sucked and sucked the more
Fruits which that unknown orchard bore;
She sucked until her lips were sore;
Then flung the emptied rinds away
But gathered up one kernel-stone,
And knew not was it night or day
As she turned home alone.   140

Lizzie met her at the gate
Full of wise upbraidings:
'Dear, you should not stay so late,
Twilight is not good for maidens;
Should not loiter in the glen
In the haunts of goblin men.
Do you not remember Jeanie,
How she met them in the moonlight,
Took their gifts both choice and many,
Ate their fruits and wore their flowers   150
Plucked from bowers
Where summer ripens at all hours?
But ever in the noonlight
She pined and pined away;
Sought them by night and day,
Found them no more but dwindled and grew grey;

Then fell with the first snow,
While to this day no grass will grow
Where she lies low:
I planted daisies there a year ago 160
That never blow.
You should not loiter so.'
'Nay, hush,' said Laura:
'Nay, hush, my sister:
I ate and ate my fill,
Yet my mouth waters still;
Tomorrow night I will
Buy more:' and kissed her:
'Have done with sorrow;
I'll bring you plums tomorrow
Fresh on their mother twigs, 170
Cherries worth getting;
You cannot think what figs
My teeth have met in,
What melons icy-cold
Piled on a dish of gold
Too huge for me to hold,
What peaches with a velvet nap,
Pellucid grapes without one seed:
Odorous indeed must be the mead 180
Whereon they grow, and pure the wave they drink
With lilies at the brink,
And sugar-sweet their sap.'

Golden head by golden head,
Like two pigeons in one nest
Folded in each other's wings,
They lay down in their curtained bed:
Like two blossoms on one stem,
Like two flakes of new-fall'n snow,
Like two wands of ivory 190
Tipped with gold for awful kings.
Moon and stars gazed in at them,
Wind sang to them a lullaby,
Lumbering owls forebore to fly,
Not a bat flapped to and fro
Round their rest:

Cheek to cheek and breast to breast
Locked together in one nest.

Early in the morning
When the first cock crowed his warning,   200
Neat like bees, as sweet and busy,
Laura rose with Lizzie:
Fetched in honey, milked the cows,
Aired and set to rights the house,
Kneaded cakes of whitest wheat,
Cakes for dainty mouths to eat,
Next churned butter, whipped up cream,
Fed their poultry, sat and sewed;
Talked as modest maidens should:
Lizzie with an open heart,
Laura in an absent dream,   210
One content, one sick in part:
One warbling for the mere bright day's delight,
One longing for the night.

At length slow evening came:
They went with pitchers to the reedy brook;
Lizzie most placid in her look,
Laura most like a leaping flame.
They drew the gurgling water from its deep;
Lizzie plucked purple and rich golden flags,   220
Then turning homewards said, 'The sunset flushes
Those furthest loftiest crags;
Come, Laura, not another maiden lags,
No wilful squirrel wags,
The beasts and birds are fast asleep.'
But Laura loitered still among the rushes
And said the bank was steep.

And said the hour was early still,
The dew not fall'n, the wind not chill:
Listening ever, but not catching   230
The customary cry,
'Come buy, come buy,'
With its iterated jingle
Of sugar-baited words:

Not for all her watching
Once discerning even one goblin
Racing, whisking, tumbling, hobbling;
Let alone the herds
That used to tramp along the glen,
In groups or single,   240
Of brisk fruit-merchant men.
Till Lizzie urged, 'O Laura, come;
I hear the fruit-call but I dare not look:
You should not loiter longer at this brook:
Come with me home.
The stars rise, the moon bends her arc,
Each glow-worm winks her spark,
Let us get home before the night grows dark:
For clouds may gather
Tho' this is summer weather,   250
Put out the lights and drench us thro';
Then if we lost our way what should we do?'

Laura turned cold as stone
To find her sister heard that cry alone,
That goblin cry,
'Come buy our fruits, come buy.'
Must she then buy no more such dainty fruit?
Must she no more such succous pasture find,
Gone deaf and blind?
Her tree of life drooped from the root: ,   260
She said not one word in her heart's sore ache:
But peering thro' the dimness, nought discerning,
Trudged home, her pitcher dripping all the way;
So crept to bed, and lay
Silent till Lizzie slept;
Then sat up in a passionate yearning,
And gnashed her teeth for baulked desire, and wept
As if her heart would break.

Day after day, night after night;
Laura kept watch in vain   270
In sullen silence of exceeding pain.
She never caught again the goblin cry:
'Come buy, come buy':

She never spied the goblin men
Hawking their fruits along the glen:
But when the moon waxed bright
Her hair grew thin and grey;
She dwindled, as the fair full moon doth turn
To swift decay and burn
Her fire away.   280

One day remembering her kernel-stone
She set it by a wall that faced the south;
Dewed it with tears, hoped for a root,
Watched for a waxing shoot,
But there came none;
It never saw the sun,
It never felt the trickling moisture run;
While with sunk eyes and faded mouth
She dreamed of melons, as a traveller sees
False waves in desert drouth   290
With shade of leaf-crowned trees,
And burns the thirstier in the sandful breeze.
She no more swept the house,
Tended the fowls or cows,
Fetched honey, kneaded cakes of wheat,
Brought water from the brook:
But sat down listless in the chimney-nook
And would not eat.

Tender Lizzie could not bear
To watch her sister's cankerous care   300
Yet not to share.
She night and morning
Caught the goblins' cry:
'Come buy our orchard fruits,
Come buy, come buy':
Beside the brook, along the glen,
She heard the tramp of goblin men,
The voice and stir
Poor Laura could not hear;
Longed to buy fruit to comfort her,   310
But feared to pay too dear.
She thought of Jeanie in her grave,

Who would have been a bride;
But who for joys brides hope to have
Fell sick and died
In her gay prime,
In earliest Winter time,
With the first glazing rime,
With the first snow-fall of crisp Winter time.

Till Laura dwindling   320
Seemed knocking at Death's door:
Then Lizzie weighed no more
Better and worse;
But put a silver penny in her purse,
Kissed Laura, crossed the heath with clumps of furze
At twilight, halted by the brook:
And for the first time in her life
Began to listen and look.

Laughed every goblin
When they spied her peeping: 330
Came towards her hobbling,
Flying, running, leaping,
Puffing and blowing,
Chuckling, clapping, crowing,
Clucking and gobbling,
Mopping and mowing,
Full of airs and graces,
Pulling wry faces,
Demure grimaces,
Cat-like and rat-like,   340
Ratel- and wombat-like
Snail-paced in a hurry,
Parrot-voiced and whistler,
Helter skelter, hurry skurry,
Chattering like magpies,
Fluttering like pigeons,
Gliding like fishes,
Hugged her and kissed her,
Squeezed and caressed her;
Stretched up their dishes,   350
Panniers and plates:

'Look at our apples
Russet and dun,
Bob at our cherries,
Bite at our peaches,
Citrons and dates,
Grapes for the asking,
Pears red with basking
Out in the sun,
Plums on their twigs;   360
Pluck them and suck them,
Pomegranates, figs.'

'Good folk,' said Lizzie,
Mindful of Jeanie:
'Give me much and many;'
Held out her apron,
Tossed them her penny.
'Nay, take a seat with us,
Honour and eat with us,'
They answered grinning: 370
'Our feast is but beginning.
Night is yet early,
Warm and dew-pearly,
Wakeful and starry:
Such fruits as these
No man can carry;
Half their bloom would fly,
Half their dew would dry,
Half their flavour would pass by.
Sit down and feast with us,   380
Be welcome guest with us,
Cheer you and rest with us.'
'Thank you,' said Lizzie: 'But one waits
At home alone for me:
So without further parleying,
If you will not sell me any
Of your fruits tho' much and many,
Give me back my silver penny
I tossed you for a fee.'
They began to scratch their pates,   390
No longer wagging, purring,

But visibly demurring,
Grunting and snarling.
One called her proud,
Cross-grained, uncivil;
Their tones waxed loud,
Their looks were evil.
Lashing their tails
They trod and hustled her,
Elbowed and jostled her,   400
Clawed with their nails,
Barking, mewing, hissing, mocking,
Tore her gown and soiled her stocking,
Twitched her hair out by the roots,
Stamped upon her tender feet,
Held her hands and squeezed their fruits
Against her mouth to make her eat.
White and golden Lizzie stood,
Like a lily in a flood,
Like a rock of blue-veined stone   410
Lashed by tides obstreperously,
Like a beacon left alone
In a hoary roaring sea,
Sending up a golden fire,
Like a fruit-crowned orange-tree
White with blossoms honey-sweet
Sore beset by wasp and bee,
Like a royal virgin town
Topped with gilded dome and spire
Close beleaguered by a fleet   420
Mad to tug her standard down.

One may lead a horse to water
Twenty cannot make him drink.
Tho' the goblins cuffed and caught her,
Coaxed and fought her,
Bullied and besought her,
Scratched her, pinched her black as ink,
Kicked and knocked her,
Mauled and mocked her,
Lizzie uttered not a word;   430
Would not open lip from lip

Lest they should cram a mouthful in:
But laughed in heart to feel the drip
Of juice that syrupped all her face,
And lodged in dimples of her chin,
And streaked her neck which quaked like curd.
At last the evil people
Worn out by her resistance
Flung back her penny, kicked their fruit
Along whichever road they took,   440
Not leaving root or stone or shoot;
Some writhed into the ground,
Some dived into the brook
With ring and ripple.
Some scudded on the gale without a sound,
Some vanished in the distance.
In a smart, ache, tingle,
Lizzie went her way;
Knew not was it night or day;
Sprang up the bank, tore thro' the furze,   450
Threaded copse and dingle,
And heard her penny jingle
Bouncing in her purse,
Its bounce was music to her ear.
She ran and ran
As if she feared some goblin man
Dogged her with gibe or curse
Or something worse:
But not one goblin scurried after,
Nor was she pricked by fear;   460
The kind heart made her windy-paced
That urged her home quite out of breath with haste
And inward laughter.

She cried, 'Laura,' up the garden,
'Did you miss me?
Come and kiss me.
Never mind my bruises,
Hug me, kiss me, suck my juices
Squeezed from goblin fruits for you,
Goblin pulp and goblin dew.   470
Eat me, drink me, love me;

Laura, make much of me:
For your sake I have braved the glen
And had to do with goblin merchant men.'

Laura started from her chair,
Flung her arms up in the air,
Clutched her hair:
'Lizzie, Lizzie, have you tasted
For my sake the fruit forbidden?
Must your light like mine be hidden,   480
Your young life like mine be wasted,
Undone in mine undoing
And ruined in my ruin,
Thirsty, cankered, goblin-ridden?'
She clung about her sister,
Kissed and kissed and kissed her:
Tears once again
Refreshed her shrunken eyes,
Dropping like rain
After long sultry drouth;   490
Shaking with aguish fear, and pain,
She kissed and kissed her with a hungry mouth.

Her lips began to scorch,
That juice was wormwood to her tongue,
She loathed the feast:
Writhing as one possessed she leaped and sung,
Rent all her robe, and wrung
Her hands in lamentable haste,
And beat her breast.
Her locks streamed like the torch   500
Borne by a racer at full speed,
Or like the mane of horses in their flight,
Or like an eagle when she stems the light
Straight toward the sun,
Or like a caged thing freed,
Or like a flying flag when armies run.

Swift fire spread thro' her veins, knocked at her heart
Met the fire smouldering there
And overbore its lesser flame;

She gorged on bitterness without a name: 510
Ah! fool, to choose such part
Of soul-consuming care!
Sense failed in the mortal strife:
Like the watch-tower of a town
Which an earthquake shatters down,
Like a lightning-stricken mast,
Like a wind-uprooted tree
Spun about,
Like a foam-topped waterspout
Cast down headlong in the sea, 520
She fell at last;
Pleasure past and anguish past,
Is it death or is it life?

Life out of death.
That night long, Lizzie watched by her,
Counted her pulse's flagging stir,
Felt for her breath,
Held water to her lips, and cooled her face
With tears and fanning leaves:
But when the first birds chirped about their eaves, 530
And early reapers plodded to the place
Of golden sheaves,
And dew-wet grass
Bowed in the morning winds so brisk to pass,
And new buds with new day
Opened of cup-like lilies on the stream,
Laura awoke as from a dream,
Laughed in the innocent old way,
Hugged Lizzie but not once or thrice;
Her gleaming locks showed not one thread of grey, 540
Her breath was sweet as May
And light danced in her eyes.

Days, weeks, months, years
Afterwards, when both were wives
With children of their own;
Their mother-hearts beset with fears,
Their lives bound up in tender lives;
Laura would call the little ones

And tell them of her early prime,
Those pleasant days long gone 550
Of not-returning time;
Would talk about the haunted glen,
The wicked, quaint fruit-merchant men,
Their fruits like honey to the throat
But poison in the blood;
(Men sell not such in any town:)
Would tell them how her sister stood,
In deadly peril to do her good,
And win the fiery antidote:
Then joining hands to little hands 560
Would bid them cling together,
'For there is no friend like a sister
In calm or stormy weather;
To cheer one on the tedious way,
To fetch one if one goes astray,
To lift one if one totters down,
To strengthen whilst one stands.'

1859

The Queen of Hearts

How comes it, Flora, that, whenever we
Play cards together, you invariably,
   However the pack parts,
Still hold the Queen of Hearts?

I've scanned you with a scrutinizing gaze,
Resolved to fathom these your secret ways:
   But, sift them as I will,
   Your ways are secret still.

I cut and shuffle; shuffle, cut, again;
But all my cutting, shuffling, proves in vain: 10
   Vain hope, vain forethought too;
   That Queen still falls to you.

I dropped her once, prepense; but, ere the deal
Was dealt, your instinct seemed her loss to feel:
   'There should be one card more,'
    You said, and searched the floor.

I cheated once; I made a private notch
In Heart-Queen's back, and kept a lynx-eyed watch;
   Yet such another back
    Deceived me in the pack: 20

The Queen of Clubs assumed by arts unknown
An imitative dint that seemed my own;
   This notch, not of my doing,
    Misled me to my ruin.

It baffles me to puzzle out the clue,
Which must be skill, or craft, or luck in you:
   Unless, indeed, it be
    Natural affinity.

                1863

Autumn Violets

Keep love for youth, and violets for the spring:
   Or if these bloom when worn-out autumn grieves,
   Let them lie hid in double shade of leaves,
Their own, and others dropped down withering;
For violets suit when home birds build and sing,
   Not when the outbound bird a passage cleaves;
   Not with dry stubble of mown harvest sheaves,
But when the green world buds to blossoming.
Keep violets for the spring, and love for youth,
   Love that should dwell with beauty, mirth, and hope: 10
    Or if a later sadder love be born,
   Let this not look for grace beyond its scope,
But give itself, nor plead for answering truth—
   A grateful Ruth,* tho' gleaning scanty corn.

                1868

A Christmas Carol

In the bleak mid-winter,
  Frosty wind made moan,
Earth stood hard as iron,
  Water like a stone;
Snow had fallen, snow on snow,
  Snow on snow,
In the bleak mid-winter
  Long ago.

Our God, Heaven cannot hold Him
  Nor earth sustain;
Heaven and earth shall flee away
  When He comes to reign:
In the bleak mid-winter
  A stable-place sufficed
The Lord God Almighty
  Jesus Christ.

Enough for Him whom cherubim
  Worship night and day,
A breastful of milk
  And a mangerful of hay;
Enough for Him whom angels
  Fall down before,
The ox and ass and camel
  Which adore.

Angels and archangels
  May have gathered there,
Cherubim and seraphim
  Thronged the air,
But only His mother
  In her maiden bliss
Worshipped the Beloved
  With a kiss.

What can I give Him,
  Poor as I am?

If I were a shepherd
  I would bring a lamb,
If I were a wise man
  I would do my part—
Yet what I can, I give Him,
  Give my heart.   40

1872

Donna Innominata

7

*'Qui primavera sempre ed ogni frutto.'**
    DANTE

*'Ragionando con meco ed io con lui.'**
    PETRARCA

'Love me, for I love you'—and answer me,
  'Love me, for I love you': so shall we stand
  As happy equals in the flowering land
Of love, that knows not a dividing sea.
Love builds the house on rock and not on sand,
  Love laughs while the winds rave desperately;
And who hath found love's citadel unmanned?
  And who hath held in bonds love's liberty?
My heart's a coward though my words are brave—
  We meet so seldom, yet we surely part   10
  So often; there's a problem for your art!
  Still I find comfort in his Book who saith,
Though jealousy be cruel as the grave,
  And death be strong, yet love is strong as death.*

before 1882

10

*'Con miglior corso e con migliore stella.'**
DANTE

*'La vita fugge e non s'arresta un' ora.'**
PETRARCA

Time flies, hope flags, life plies a wearied wing;
   Death following hard on life gains ground apace.
   Faith runs with each and rears an eager face,
Out runs the rest, makes light of everything,
Spurns earth, and still finds breath to pray and sing;
   While love ahead of all uplifts his praise,
   Still asks for grace and still gives thanks for grace,
Content with all day brings and night will bring.
Life wanes; and when love folds his wings above
   Tired hope, and less we feel his conscious pulse,   10
   Let us go fall asleep, dear friend, in peace;
   A little while, and age and sorrow cease;
   A little while, and life reborn annuls
Loss and decay and death, and all is love.

before 1882

11

*'Vien dietro a me e lascia dir le genti.'**
DANTE

*'Contando i casi della vita nostra.'**
PETRARCA

Many in aftertimes will say of you
   'He loved her'—while of me what will they say?
   Not that I loved you more than just in play,
For fashion's sake as idle women do.
Even let them prate; who know not what we knew
   Of love and parting in exceeding pain,
   Of parting hopeless here to meet again,
Hopeless on earth, and heaven is out of view,
But by my heart of love laid bare to you,
   My love that you can make not void nor vain,   10
Love that foregoes you but to claim anew

Beyond this passage of the gate of death,
  I charge you at the Judgment make it plain
My love of you was life and not a breath.

before 1882

12

'Amor che ne la mente mi ragiona.'*
                 Dante

'Amor vien nel bel viso di costei.'*
                 Petrarca

If there be anyone can take my place
  And make you happy whom I grieve to grieve,
  Think not that I can grudge it, but believe
I do commend you to that nobler grace,
That readier wit than mine, that sweeter face;
  Yea, since your riches make me rich, conceive
  I too am crowned, while bridal crowns I weave,
And thread the bridal dance with jocund pace.
For if I did not love you, it might be
  That I should grudge you some one dear delight;   10
  But since the heart is yours that was mine own,
  Your pleasure is my pleasure, right my right,
Your honourable freedom makes me free,
  And you companioned I am not alone.

before 1882

14

'E la Sua Volontade è nostra pace.'*
                 Dante

'Sol con questi pensier, con altre chiome.'*
                 Petrarca

Youth gone, and beauty gone if ever there
  Dwelt beauty in so poor a face as this;
  Youth gone and beauty, what remains of bliss?
I will not bind fresh roses in my hair,
To shame a cheek at best but little fair,
  Leave youth his roses, who can bear a thorn,—

I will not seek for blossoms anywhere,
   Except such common flowers as blow with corn.
Youth gone and beauty gone, what doth remain?
   The longing of a heart pent up forlorn,   10
   A silent heart whose silence loves and longs;
   The silence of a heart which sang its songs
   While youth and beauty made a summer morn,
Silence of love that cannot sing again.

                              before 1882

A Woman's Question

Before I trust my Fate to thee,
  Or place my hand in thine,
Before I let thy Future give
  Colour and form to mine,
Before I peril all for thee, question thy soul tonight for me.

I break all slighter bonds, nor feel
  A shadow of regret:
Is there one link within the Past,
  That holds thy spirit yet?
Or is thy Faith as clear and free as that which I can pledge
    to thee?   10

Does there within thy dimmest dreams
  A possible future shine,
Wherein thy life could henceforth breathe,
  Untouched, unshared by mine?
If so, at any pain or cost, oh, tell me before all is lost.

Look deeper still. If thou canst feel
  Within thy inmost soul,
That thou hast kept a portion back,
  While I have staked the whole;
Let no false pity spare the blow, but in true mercy tell me
    so.   20

Is there within thy heart a need
  That mine cannot fulfil?
One chord that any other hand
  Could better wake or still?
Speak now—lest at some future day my whole life wither
    and decay.

Lives there within thy nature hid
  The demon-spirit Change,
Shedding a passing glory still
  On all things new and strange?—
It may not be thy fault alone—but shield my heart against
    thy own.   30

Couldst thou withdraw thy hand one day
  And answer to my claim,
That Fate, and that today's mistake,
  Not thou—had been to blame?
Some soothe their conscience thus: but thou wilt surely
    warn and save me now.

Nay, answer *not*—I dare not hear,
  The words would come too late;
Yet I would spare thee all remorse,
  So, comfort thee, my Fate—
Whatever on my heart may fall—remember, I *would* risk
    it all!   40

1858

A Love Token

Do you grieve no costly offering
  To the Lady you can make?
One there is, and gifts less worthy
  Queens have stooped to take.

Take a Heart of virgin silver,
  Fashion it with heavy blows,
Cast it into Love's hot furnace
  When it fiercest glows.

With Pain's sharpest point transfix it,
  And then carve in letters fair,   10
Tender dreams and quaint devices,
  Fancies sweet and rare.

Set within it Hope's blue sapphire,
   Many-changing opal fears,
Blood-red ruby-stones of daring,
   Mixed with pearly tears.

And when you have wrought and laboured
   Till the gift is all complete,
You may humbly lay your offering
   At the Lady's feet.   20

Should her mood perchance be gracious—
   With disdainful smiling pride,
She will place it with the trinkets
   Glittering at her side.

1858

Rhymes for the Times

2

Ae day short syne, whan gaun afiel,
A douce aul' farrant eldrin chiel
Cam' yont the burn tae hae a crack,
For John an' me hae lang been pack.
Quo he, Thir's unco times we leeve in,
There's muckle dune, ance past believin'.
Hae ye no heard in Glasgow College
They've plantit a new tree o' knowledge?
The frute's fu' bonny to the e'e,
An' woman's no forbid tae pree: 10
Sae she may cum without presumption,
An' pu' an' eat an' gather gumption.
An' sic lang-wint, lang-nebbit cracks,
'Bout social rights, an' wrangs, an' facts,
Frae chiels wi' tongues sae glib an' snell,
They tingilit thro' ye like a bell.
There's mony a phase o' speech an' thocht,
Leuks gran', but whan it's to be wrocht,
An' practice, 'stead o' speech begins,
There's stumlin'-blocks to break oor shins,   20
Ower whilk we'll stacher, stoit, an' tummle,
Syne juist sit doon an' glunch an' grumil.
Speech is a tree that bears nae frute,
Till delvit and dungit aboot the rute.
The yird weel loosit an' labourit, syne
Leuk for a crap, baith big and fine,
Whan words an' wark mak' firm alliance,
Then social duty's social science.

    An' noo that we hae dune wi' speakin',
Fie let us to the wark be streekin'.   30
Aff wi' yer coat, up wi' yer sleeves,

Set doon yer feet, an' ply yer neives.
On, on, nae stannin' still, nor jaukin,
Oor wark's ahin, hae dune wi' taukin';
For that's ane o' the richts o' woman,
I houp her gude time's nearer comin'—
Hech, there's a warl o' wark afore her,
An' Heaven an' yirth are leukin' o'er her.
Noo, John, quo I, haud aff oor taes,
A woman best kens woman's ways: 40
There's ae thing she can hardly name,
A thing o' filth, an' sin, an' shame;
To chack that ugsume kin' o' sinnin',
She maun begin at the beginnin'.
Nae lassie ere was born on yirth,
But Nature gied her, at her birth,
A shrinkin', shame-faced, modest pride,
Her baith as bairn an' maid to guide.
O mithers, guard this precious sense—
This bashfu' modesty and mense,   50
Sae sweet, but oh, ower scarce to see!
Yer warnin' words, an' watchfu' e'e,
Sood never lea' them lang their lanes,
Wi' ill brocht up, ill deedie weans.
An' cleed their limbs wi' decent claes,
A gey bit nearer to the taes,
An' aye the guileless bonny burds
Keep frae a' shamefu' sichts an' words.
Ay, mithers, ye hae muckle mair
To gie yer bairns than schulin' lear;   60
At schule ye like to see them braw,
Wi' peenie white as drifted snaw,
An' hoopit coatie, short an' wide,
An' curls that hing on ilka side
O rosy cheeks an' lauchin een,
An' a' aboot them snod an' clean.
This ye may dae, but let the min'
An' wee bit hertie, saft an' kin',
The mither's anxious luve an' care,
An' eident teachin' foremaist share,   70
An' let yer cares aye deeper grup
Whan they to maidhood are grown up,

An' tho' the wark war ne'er sae thrang,
Ken wha they're wi', an' whaur they gang
Be to yer duty leal an' true,
An' sood ye fail, nae blame to you.

There's been an unco tauk an' fyke
'Boot women's wark, an' things sic like.
The shooster lasses, save the mark!
They say sood hae the shopmen's wark,   80
An' sort the teeps, an' wield the pen,
An' blackleg on the workin' men.
An' sood they get the pay an' place
Men used to hae, they'll hae the grace
By their glib mouth-piece Bessie Park,*
To tell the chiels whaur they'll get wark;
They canna dig, to beg think shame,
They'll list, or seek a foreign hame.
Noo, lasses, I wad hae ye ken,
To herry oot the nice young men   90
Is no' the gate to win their favour.
By thrifty, modest, quiet behaviour,
A wheen o' ye micht aiblins share
A' that they wurk for evermair.
An' are we cum to sic a pass
That wark, an' meat, for mony a lass,
Can no' be had in oor bit islan',
But by her health or morals spoilin'?
Then let ilk toun oot thro' the nation
Subscribe for female emigration,   100
To tak' them far frae wants an' harms,
To lan's whaur woman's presence charms
An' blesses men, whase lanely lives
An' lanely hames hae need o' wives.

Ae word to speechifyin' weemen,
That's no aye sleepin' whan they're dreamin',
Aye takin' up puir woman's quarrels,
Let your first care be woman's morals;
For social ills, an' deeds impure,
Prevention easier is than cure.   110
Help mithers wi' their maiden charge,

Help lassies coosten oot at large
Upon a warl' baith caul an' stern,
Wi' muckle baith to thole and learn.
An' since ye've time an' win' to spare,
Them baith on sister woman ware,
To touch her heart an' teach her saul,
This mission's yours—obey the call.

1863

GEORGE ELIOT

In a London Drawingroom

The sky is cloudy, yellowed by the smoke.
For view there are the houses opposite
Cutting the sky with one long line of wall
Like solid fog: far as the eye can stretch
Monotony of surface and of form
Without a break to hang a guess upon.
No bird can make a shadow as it flies,
For all its shadow, as in ways o'erhung
By thickest canvas, where the golden rays
Are clothed in hemp. No figure lingering   10
Pauses to feed the hunger of the eye
Or rest a little on the lap of life.
All hurry on and look upon the ground,
Or glance unmarking at the passers by.
The wheels are hurrying too, cabs, carriages
All closed, in multiplied identity.
The world seems one huge prison-house and court
Where men are punished at the slightest cost,
With lowest rate of colour, warmth and joy.

1865

Brother and Sister*

I

I cannot choose but think upon the time
When our two lives grew like two buds that kiss
At lightest thrill from the bee's swinging chime,
Because the one so near the other is.

He was the elder and a little man
Of forty inches, bound to show no dread,
And I the girl that puppy-like now ran,
Now lagged behind my brother's larger tread.

I held him wise, and when he talked to me
Of snakes and birds, and which God loved the best,   10
I thought his knowledge marked the boundary
Where men grew blind, though angels knew the rest.

    If he said 'Hush!' I tried to hold my breath
    Wherever he said 'Come!' I stepped in faith.

2

Long years have left their writing on my brow,
But yet the freshness and the dew-fed beam
Of those young mornings are about me now,
When we two wandered toward the far-off stream

With rod and line. Our basket held a store
Baked for us only, and I thought with joy
That I should have my share, though he had more,
Because he was the elder and a boy.

The firmaments of daisies since to me
Have had those mornings in their opening eyes,   10
The bunchèd cowslip's pale transparency
Carries that sunshine of sweet memories.

    And wild-rose branches take their finest scent
    From those blest hours of infantine content.

3

Our mother bade us keep the trodden ways,
Stroked down my tippet, set my brother's frill,
Then with the benediction of her gaze
Clung to us lessening, and pursued us still

Across the homestead to the rookery elms,
Whose tall old trunks had each a grassy mound,
So rich for us, we counted them as realms
With varied products: here were earth-nuts found,

And here the Lady-fingers in deep shade;
Here sloping toward the Moat the rushes grew,   10
The large to split for pith, the small to braid;
While over all the dark rooks cawing flew.

   And made a happy strange solemnity,
   A deep-toned chant from the unknown to me.

4

Our meadow-path had memorable spots:
One where it bridged a tiny rivulet,
Deep hid my tangled blue Forget-me-nots;
And all along the waving grasses met

My little palm, or nodded to my cheek,
When flowers with upturned faces gazing drew
My wonder downward, seeming all to speak
With eyes of souls that dumbly heard and knew.

Then came the copse, where wild things rushed unseen,
And black-scathed grass betrayed the past abode   10
Of mystic gypsies, who still lurked between
Me and each hidden distance of the road.

   A gypsy once had startled me at play,
   Blotting with her dark smile my sunny day.

5

Thus rambling we were schooled in deepest lore,
And learned the meanings that give words a soul,
The fear, the love, the primal passionate store,
Whose shaping impulses make manhood whole.

Those hours were seed to all my after good;
My infant gladness, through eye, ear, and touch,
Took easily as warmth a various food
To nourish the sweet skill of loving much.

For who in age shall roam the earth and find
Reasons for loving that will strike out love   10
With sudden rod from the hard year-pressed mind?
Were reasons sown as thick as stars above,

   'Tis love must see them, as the eye sees light:
   Day is but Number to the darkened sight.

6

Our brown canal was endless to my thought;
And on its banks I sat in dreamy peace,
Unknowing how the good I loved was wrought,
Untroubled by the fear that it would cease

Slowly the barges floated into view
Rounding a grassy hill to me sublime
With some Unknown beyond it, whither flew
The parting cuckoo toward a fresh spring time.

The wide-arched bridge, the scented elder-flowers,
The wondrous watery rings that died too soon,   10
The echoes of the quarry, the still hours
With white robe sweeping-on the shadeless noon.

   Were but my growing self, are part of me,
   My present Past, my root of piety.

7

Those long days measured by my little feet
Had chronicles which yield me many a text;
Where irony still finds an image meet
Of full grown judgments in this world perplext.

One day my brother left me in high charge,
To mind the rod, while he went seeking bait,
And bade me, when I saw a nearing barge,
Snatch out the line, lest he should come too late.

Proud of the task, I watched with all my might
For one whole minute, till my eyes grew wide,   10
Till sky and earth took on a strange new light
And seemed a dream-world floating on some tide—

   A fair pavilioned boat for me alone
   Bearing me onward through the vast unknown.

8

But sudden came the barge's pitch-black prow,
Nearer and angrier came my brother's cry,
And all my soul was quivering fear, when lo!
Upon the imperilled line, suspended high,

A silver perch! My guilt that won the prey,
Now turned to merit, had a guerdon rich
Of hugs and praises, and made merry play,
Until my triumph reached its highest pitch

When all at home were told the wondrous feat,
And how the little sister had fished well.   10
In secret, though my fortune tasted sweet,
I wondered why this happiness befell.

   'The little lass had luck,' the gardener said:
   And so I learned, luck was with glory wed.

9

We had the self-same world enlarged for each
By loving difference of girl and boy:
The fruit that hung on high beyond my reach
He plucked for me, and oft he must employ

A measuring glance to guide my tiny shoe
Where lay firm stepping-stones, or call to mind
'This thing I like my sister may not do,
For she is little, and I must be kind.'

Thus boyish Will the nobler mastery learned
Where inward vision over impulse reigns,   10
Widening its life with separate life discerned,
A Like unlike, a Self that self restrains.

  His years with others must the sweeter be
  For those brief days he spent in loving me.

                    10

His sorrow was my sorrow, and his joy
Sent little leaps and laughs through all my frame;
My doll seemed lifeless and no girlish toy
Had any reason when my brother came.

I knelt with him at marbles, marked his fling
Cut the ringed stem and make the apple drop,
Or watched him winding close the spiral string
That looped the orbits of the humming top.

Grasped by such fellowship my vagrant thought
Ceased with dream-fruit dream-wishes to fulfil;   10
My aery-picturing fantasy was taught
Subjection to the harder, truer skill

  That seeks with deeds to grave a thought-tracked line,
  And by 'What is', 'What will be' to define.

                    11

School parted us; we never found again
That childish world where our two spirits mingled
Like scents from varying roses that remain
One sweetness, nor can evermore be singled.

Yet the twin habit of that early time
Lingered for long about the heart and tongue:
We had been natives of one happy clime,
And its dear accent to our utterance clung.

Till the dire years whose awful name is Change
Had grasped our souls still yearning in divorce, 10
And pitiless shaped them in two forms that range
Two elements which sever their life's course.

But were another childhood-world my share,
I would be born a little sister there.

1869

The Weary Spinnin O't

Sittin spinnin, sittin spinnin
  A' the lea-lang day,
Hearin the bit burnie rinnin,
  And the bairns at play.
I'm sweir to get my leg let loose,
To do a turn about the hoose;
Oh, amna I a waefu wife
To spin awa my threid of life?
Spinnin, spinnin, ever spinnin,
Never endin, aye beginnin;   10
Hard at wark wi hand and fuit,
Oh, the weary spinnin o't!

Sittin spinnin, sittin spinnin
  Vow but I am thrang,
My wee pickle siller winnin,
  Croonin some auld sang.
Leese me o my spinnin-wheel,
Gie's us a' oor milk and meal;
Weet or dry, or het or cauld,
I maun spin till I grow auld.   20
Spinnin, spinnin, ever spinnin,
Never endin, aye beginnin,
Hard at wark wi hand and fuit
At the weary spinnin o't.

Sittin spinnin, sitting spinnin,
  Sic a wear and tear,
Tabs of tow for wabs o linen,
  Till my heid is sair.
Mony a wiselike wab I've spun,
Spreid and sortit i the sun;   30
Puirtith cauld is ill to bear;

Mony bairns bring mickle care.
Spinnin, spinnin, ever spinnin,
Never endin, aye beginnin,
Hard at wark wi hand and fuit,
Oh! the weary spinnin o't!

1873

ALICE MEYNELL

Renouncement

I must not think of thee; and, tired yet strong,
   I shun the thought that lurks in all delight—
   The thought of thee—and in the blue Heaven's height,
And in the sweet passage of a song.
Oh, just beyond the fairest thoughts that throng
   This breast, the thought of thee waits, hidden yet bright;
   But it must never, never come in sight;
I must stop short of thee the whole day long.

But when sleep comes to close each difficult day,
   When night gives pause to the long watch I keep,   10
     And all my bonds I needs must loose apart,
Must doff my will as raiment laid away,—
   With the first dream that comes with the first sleep
   I run, I run, I am gathered to thy heart.

1875

The Poet to His Childhood

In my thought I see you stand with a path on either hand,
—Hills that look into the sun, and there a rivered meadow-land.
And your lost voice with the things that it decreed across me
   thrills,
   When you thought, and chose the hills.

'If it prove a life of pain, greater have I judged the gain.
With a singing soul for music's sake, I climb and meet the rain,
And I choose, whilst I am calm, my thought and labouring to be
   Unconsoled by sympathy.'

'But how dared you use me so? For you bring my ripe years low
To your child's whim and a destiny your child-soul could not
    know.   10
And that small voice legislating I revolt against, with tears.
  But you mark not, through the years.

'To the mountain leads my way. If the plains are green today,
These my barren hills are flushing faintly, strangely, in the May,
With the presence of the Spring amongst the smallest flowers that
    grow.'
  But the summer in the snow?

Do you know, who are so bold, how in sooth the rule will hold,
Settled by a wayward child's ideal at some ten years old?
—How the human hearts you slip from, thoughts and love you
    stay not for,
  Will not open to you more?   20

You were rash then, little child, for the skies with storms are wild,
And you faced the dim horizon with its whirl of mists, and smiled,
Climbed a little higher, lonelier, in the solitary sun,
  To feel how the winds came on.

But your sunny silence there, solitude so light to bear,
Will become a long dumb world up in the colder sadder air,
And the little mournful lonelinesses in the little hills
  Wider wilderness fulfils.

And if e'er you should come down to the village or the town,
With the cold rain for your garland, and the wind for your
    renown,   30
You will stand upon the thresholds with a face of dumb desire,
  Nor be known by any fire.

It is the memory that shrinks. You were all too brave, methinks,
Climbing solitudes of flowering cistus and the thin wild pinks,
Musing, setting to a haunting air in one vague reverie
  All the life that was to be.

With a smile do I complain in the safety of the pain,
Knowing that my feet can never quit their solitudes again;
But regret may turn with longing to that one hour's choice you
    had
  Where the silence broodeth sad.   40

I rebel *not*, child gone by, but obey you wonderingly,
For you knew not, young rash speaker, all you spoke, and now
    will I,
With the life, and all the loneliness revealed that you thought fit,
  Sing the Amen, knowing it.

                                                        1875

EDITH NESBIT

Vies Manquées*

A year ago we walked the wood—
    A year ago today;
A blackbird fluttered round her brood
    Deep in the white-flowered may.

We trod the happy woodland ways,
    Where sunset streamed between
The hazel stems in long dusk rays,
    And turned to gold the green.

A thrush sang where the ferns uncurled;
    And clouds of wind-flowers grew: 10
I missed the meaning of the world
    From lack of love for you.

You missed the beauty of the year,
    And failed its self to see,
Through too much doubt and too much fear,
    And too much love of me.

This year we hear the birds' glad strain,
    Again the sunset glows,
We walk the wild wet woods again,
    Again the wind-flower blows.   20

In cloudy white the falling may
    Drifts down the scented wind,
And so the secret drifts away
    Which we shall never find.

Our drifted spirits are not free
    Spring's secret springs to touch,
For now you do not care for me,
    And I love you too much.

1876

The Wife of All Ages

I do not catch these subtle shades of feeling,
    Your fine distinctions are too fine for me;
This meeting, scheming, longing, trembling, dreaming,
    To me mean love, and only love, you see;
In me at least 'tis love, you will admit,
And you the only man who wakens it.

Suppose *I* yearned, and longed, and dreamed, and fluttered,
    What would you say or think, or further, do?
Why should one rule be fit for me to follow,
    While there exists a different law for you?   10
If all these fires and fancies came my way,
Would you believe love was so far away?

On all these other women—never doubt it—
    'Tis love you lavish, love you promised me!
What do I care to be the first, or fiftieth?
    It is the *only one* I care to be.
Dear, I would be your sun, as mine you are,
Not the most radiant wonder of a star.

And so, good-bye! Among such sheaves of roses
    You will not miss the flower I take from you;   20
Amid the music of so many voices
    You will forget the little songs I knew—
The foolish tender words I used to say,
The little common sweets of everyday.

The world, no doubt, has fairest fruit and blossoms
    To give to you; but what, ah! what for me?
Nay, after all I am your slave and bondmaid,
    And all my world is in my slavery.
So, as before, I welcome any part
Which you may choose to give me of your heart.   30

1886

Over and Undone

If one might hope that when we say farewell
  To life, we two might but be one at last!
  But we look back on a divided past,
And a divided future must foretell.
Apart we sowed the seed that flowers in hell,
  The seed that blooms in heaven apart we cast:
  See what remembrances my heart holds fast
Ask your own heart what deeds you deem done well!

The memory I find my heaven in
Is that one hand-touch you regret as sin;   10
Your goodness, dear, that stood between us two
And made my hell, may make a heaven for you;
So evermore must lie our souls between
The kiss unkissed, the infinite might-have-been!

                                        1886

January

While yet the air is keen, and no bird sings,
  Nor any vaguest thrills of heart declare
  The presence of the springtime in the air,
Through the raw dawn the shepherd homeward brings
The wee white lambs—the little helpless things—
  For shelter, warmth, and comfortable care.
  Without his help how hardly lambs would fare—
How hardly live through winter's hours to spring's!

So let me tend and minister apart
  To my new hope, which some day you shall know: 10
It could not live in January wind
  Of your disdain; but when within your heart
  The bud and bloom of tenderness shall grow,
Amid the flowers my hope may welcome find.

                                        1886

Song

We loved, my love, and now it seems
　　Our love has brought to birth
Friendship, the fairest child of dreams,
　　The rarest gift of earth.

Soon die love's roses fresh and frail,
　　And when their bloom is o'er,
Not all our heart-wrung tears avail
　　To give them life once more.

But when true love with friendship lives,
　　As now, for thee and me,　　　　　　　　　　10
Love brings the roses—Friendship gives
　　The immortality.

　　　　　　　　　　1886

Love and Knowledge

Though you and I so long have been so near—
　　Have felt each other's heart-beats hour by hour,
　　Have watered, plucked, and trampled passion's flower,
Have known so many days so very dear—
Yet still through every hour of every year
　　We have sought to win and failed to win the dower
　　Of perfect insight, and to gain the power
To see what we are, and not what we appear.

Yet you desire such knowledge—would possess,
　　You say, completion of love; if that were won　　10
　　—Ah! by it might not haply be undone
The little measure of joy we knew before?
　　Though we should swear we love each other more,
How surely we should love each other less!

　　　　　　　　　　1886

The Claim

Oh! I admit I'm dull and poor,
   And plain and gloomy, as you tell me;
And dozens flock around your door
   Who in all points but one excel me.

You smile on them, on me you frown,
   They worship for the wage you pay;
I lay life, love and honour down
   For you to walk on every day.

I am the only one who sees
   That though such gifts can never move you,   10
A meagre price are gifts like these
   For life's high privilege—to love you.

I am the one among your train
   Who sees that loving you is worth
A thousand times the certain gain
   Of all the heaped-up joys of earth.

And you, who know as well as I,
   What your glass tells you every morning—
A kindred soul you should descry,
   Dilute with sympathy your scorning.   20

At least you should approve the intense
   Love that gives all for you to waste;
Your other lovers have more sense,
   Admit that I have better taste.

1895

Love Versus Learning

Alas for the blight of my fancies!
  Alas, for the fall of my pride!
I planned, in my girlish romances,
  To be a philosopher's bride.

I pictured him learned and witty,
  The sage and the lover combined,
Not scorning to say I was pretty,
  Nor only adoring my *mind*.

No elderly, spectacled Mentor,
  But one who would worship and woo;
Perhaps I might take an inventor,
  Or even a poet would do.

And tender and gay and well-favoured,
  My fate overtook me at last:
I saw, and I heard, and I wavered,
  I smiled, and my freedom was past.

He promised to love me forever,
  He pleaded, and what could I say?
I thought he must surely be clever,
  For he is an Oxford MA.

But now, I begin to discover
  My visions are fatally marred;
Perfection itself as a lover,
  He's neither a sage nor a bard.

He's mastered the usual knowledge,
  And says it's a terrible bore;
He formed his opinions at college,
  Then why should he think any more?

My logic he sets at defiance,
   Declares that my Latin's no use,   30
And when I begin to talk Science
   He calls me a dear little goose.

He says that my lips are too rosy
   To speak in a language that's dead,
And all that is dismal and prosy
   Should fly from so sunny a head.

He scoffs at each grave occupation,
   Turns everything off with a pun;
And says that his sole calculation
   Is how to make two into one.   40

He says Mathematics may vary,
   Geometry cease to be true,
But scorning the slightest vagary
   He still will continue to woo.

He says that the sun may stop action,
   But he will not swerve from his course;
For love is his law of attraction,
   A smile his centripetal force.

His levity's truly terrific,
   And often I think we must part,   50
But compliments so scientific
   Recapture my fluttering heart.

Yet sometimes 'tis very confusing,
   This conflict of love and of lore—
But hark! I must cease from my musing,
   For that is his knock at the door!

1881

The New Orthodoxy

So, dear Fred, you're not content
Though I quote the books you lent,
And I've kept that spray you sent
   Of the milk-white heather;
For you fear I'm too 'advanced'
To remember all that chanced
In the old days, when we danced,
   Walked, and rode together.

Trust me, Fred, beneath the curls
Of the most 'advanced' of girls,   10
Many a foolish fancy whirls,
   Bidding Fact defiance,
And the simplest village maid
Needs not to be much afraid
Of her sister, sage and staid,
   Bachelor of Science.

Ah! while yet our hope was new
Guardians thought 'twould never do
That Sir Frederick's heir should woo
   Little Amy Merton: 20
So the budding joy they snatched
From our hearts, so meetly matched—
You to Oxford they despatched,
   Me they sent to Girton.

Were the vows all writ in dust?
No—you're one-and-twenty—just—
And you write—'We will, we must
   Now, at once, be married!'
Nay, you plan the wedding trip!
Softly, sir! there's many a slip   30
Ere the goblet to the lip
   Finally is carried.

Oh, the wicked tales I hear!
Not that you at Ruskin jeer,

Nor that at Carlyle you sneer,
  With his growls dyspeptic:
But that, having read in vain
Huxley, Tyndall, Clifford, Bain,
All the scientific train—
  You're a hardened sceptic!   40

Things with fin, and claw, and hoof
Join to give us perfect proof
That our being's warp and woof
  We from near and far win;
Yet your flippant doubts you vaunt,
And—to please a maiden aunt—
You've been heard to say you can't
  Pin your faith to Darwin!

Then you jest, because Laplace*
Said this Earth was nought but gas   50
Till the vast rotating mass
  Denser grew and denser:
Something worse they whisper too,
But I'm sure it *can't* be true—
For they tell me, Fred, that you
  Scoff at Herbert Spencer!*

Write—or telegraph—or call!
Come yourself and tell me all:
No fond hope shall me enthrall,
  No regret shall sway me: 60
Yet—until the worst is said,
Till I know your faith is dead,
I remain, dear doubting Fred,
  Your believing
        Amy.

1887

Natural Selection

I had found out a gift for my fair,
   I had found where the cave-men were laid;
Skull, femur, and pelvis were there,
   And spears, that of silex they made.

But he ne'er could be true, she averred,
   Who would dig up an ancestor's grave—
And I loved her the more when I heard
   Such filial regard for the Cave.

My shelves, they are furnished with stones
   All sorted and labelled with care,   10
And a splendid collection of bones,
   Each one of them ancient and rare;

One would think she might like to retire
   To my study—she calls it a 'hole'!
Not a fossil I heard her admire,
   But I begged it, or borrowed, or stole.

But there comes an idealess lad,
   With a strut, and a stare, and a smirk;
And I watch, scientific though sad,
   The Law of Selection at work.   20

Of Science he hasn't a trace,
   He seeks not the How and the Why,
But he sings with an amateur's grace,
   And he dances much better than I.

And we know the more dandified males
   By dance and by song win their wives—
'Tis a law that with *Aves** prevails,
   And even in *Homo** survives.

Shall I rage as they twirl in the valse?
   Shall I sneer as they carol and coo?   30
Ah no! for since Chloë is false,
   I'm certain that Darwin is true!

1887

A Town Garden

A plot of ground—the merest scrap—
    Deep like a dry, forgotten well,
A garden caught in a brick-built trap,
    Where men make money, buy and sell;
And struggling through the stagnant haze,
    Dim flowers, with sapless leaf and stem,
Look up with something of the gaze
    That homesick eyes have cast on them.

There is a rose against the wall,
    With scanty, smoke-encrusted leaves;   10
Fair showers on happier roses fall—
    On this, foul droppings from the eaves.
It pines, but you need hardly note;
    It dies by inches in the gloom;
Shoots in the spring-time, as if by rote;
    Long has forgotten to dream of bloom.

The poorest blossom, and it were classed
    With colour and name—but never a flower!
It blooms with the roses whose bloom is past,
    Of every hue, and place, and hour.   20
They live before me as I look—
    The damask buds that breathe and glow,
Pink wild roses, down by a brook,
    Lavish clusters of airy snow.

Could one transplant you—(far on high
    A murky sunset lights the tiles)—
And set you 'neath the arching sky,
    In the green country, many miles,
Would you strike deep and suck up strength,
    Washed with rain and hung with pearls,   30

Cling to the trellis, a leafy length,
 Sweet with blossom for June and girls?

Yet no! Who needs you in these bowers?
 Who prizes gifts that all can give?
Bestow your life instead of flowers,
 And slowly die that dreams may live.
Prisoned and perishing, your dole
 Of lingering leaves shall not be vain—
Worthy to wreathe the hemlock bowl,
 Or twine about the cross of pain!   40

1883

Sonnet

'Have not all songs been sung—all loves been told?
What shall I say when nought is left unsaid?
The world is full of memories of the dead—
Echoes and relics. Here's no virgin gold,
But all assayed, none left for me to mould
Into new coin, and at your feet to shed;
Each piece is mint-marked with some poet's head,
Tested and rung in tributes manifold.

Oh for a single word should be mine own,
And not the homage of long-studied art,   10
Common to all, for you who stand apart!
Oh weariness of measures tried and known!
Yet in their rhythm, you—if you alone—
Should hear the passionate pulses of my heart!'

1888

A Minor Poet

> '*What should such fellows as I do,*
> *Crawling between heaven and earth?*'*

Here is the phial; here I turn the key
Sharp in the lock. Click!—there's no doubt it turned.
This is the third time; there is luck in threes—
Queen Luck, that rules the world, befriend me now
And freely I'll forgive you many wrongs!
Just as the draught began to work, first time,
Tom Leigh, my friend (as friends go in the world),
Burst in, and drew the phial from my hand,
(Ah, Tom! ah, Tom! that was a sorry turn!)
And lectured me a lecture, all compact
Of neatest, newest phrases, freshly culled   10
From works of newest culture: 'common good';
'The world's great harmonies'; 'must be content
With knowing God works all things for the best,
And Nature never stumbles.' Then again,
'The common good', and still, 'the common good';
And what a small thing was our joy or grief
When weighed with that of thousands. Gentle Tom,
But you might wag your philosophic tongue
From morn till eve, and still the thing's the same:
I am myself, as each man is himself—   20
Feels his own pain, joys his own joy, and loves
With his own love, no other's. Friend, the world
Is but one man; one man is but the world.
And I am I, and you are Tom, that bleeds
When needles prick your flesh (mark, yours, not mine).
I must confess it; I can feel the pulse
A-beating at my heart, yet never knew
The throb of cosmic pulses. I lament
The death of youth's ideal in my heart;
And, to be honest, never yet rejoiced   30

In the world's progress—scarce, indeed, discerned;
(For still it seems that God's a Sisyphus*
With the world for stone).
                You shake your head. I'm base,
Ignoble? Who is noble—you or I?
I was not once thus? Ah, my friend, we are
As the Fates make us.
             This time is the third;
The second time the flask fell from my hand,
Its drowsy juices spilt upon the board;
And there my face fell flat, and all the life
Crept from my limbs, and hand and foot were bound   40
With mighty chains, subtle, intangible;
While still the mind held to its wonted use,
Or rather grew intense and keen with dread,
An awful dread—I thought I was in Hell.
In Hell, in Hell! Was ever Hell conceived
By mortal brain, by brain Divine devised,
Darker, more fraught with torment, than the world
For such as I? A creature maimed and marred
From very birth. A blot, a blur, a note
All out of tune in this world's instrument.   50
A base thing, yet not knowing to fulfil
Base functions. A high thing, yet all unmeet
For work that's high. A dweller on the earth,
Yet not content to dig with other men
Because of certain sudden sights and sounds
(Bars of broke music; furtive, fleeting glimpse
Of angel faces 'thwart the grating seen)
Perceived in Heaven. Yet when I approach
To catch the sound's completeness, to absorb
The faces' full perfection, Heaven's gate,   60
Which then had stood ajar, sudden falls to,
And I, ashiver in the dark and cold,
Scarce hear afar the mocking tones of men:
'He would not dig, forsooth; but he must strive
For higher fruits than what our tillage yields;
Behold what comes, my brothers, of vain pride!'
Why play with figures? trifle prettily
With this my grief which very simply's said,
'There is no place for me in all the world'?

The world's a rock, and I will beat no more   70
A breast of flesh and blood against a rock . . .
A stride across the planks for old time's sake.

Ah, bare, small room that I have sorrowed in;
Ay, and on sunny days, haply, rejoiced;
We know some things together, you and I!
Hold there, you ranged row of books! In vain
You beckon from your shelf. You've stood my friends
Where all things else were foes; yet now I'll turn
My back upon you, even as the world
Turns it on me. And yet—farewell, farewell!   80
You, lofty Shakespeare, with the tattered leaves
And fathomless great heart, your binding's bruised
Yet did I love you less? Goethe, farewell;
Farewell, triumphant smile and tragic eyes,
And pitiless world-wisdom!
                              For all men
These two. And 'tis farewell with you, my friends;
More dear because more near; Theocritus;*
Heine that stings and smiles; Prometheus' bard;*
(I've grown too coarse for Shelley latterly:)
And one wild singer of today, whose song   90
Is all aflame with passionate bard's blood
Lashed into foam by pain and the world's wrong.
At least, he has a voice to cry his pain;
For him, no silent writhing in the dark,
No muttering of mute lips, no straining out
Of a weak throat a-choke with pent-up sound,
A-throb with pent-up passion . . .
                              Ah, my sun!
That's you, then, at the window, looking in
To beam farewell on one who's loved you long
And very truly. Up, you creaking thing,   100
You squinting, cobwebbed casement!
                              So, at last,
I can drink in the sunlight. How it falls
Across that endless sea of London roofs,
Weaving such golden wonders on the grey,
That almost, for the moment, we forget
The world of woe beneath them.

           Underneath,
For all the sunset glory, Pain is king.
Yet, the sun's there, and very sweet withal;
And I'll not grumble that it's only sun,
But open wide my lips—thus—drink it in;   110
Turn up my face to the sweet evening sky
(What royal wealth of scarlet on the blue
So tender toned, you'd almost think it green)
And stretch my hands out—so—to grasp it tight.
Ha, ha! 'tis sweet awhile to cheat the Fates,
And be as happy as another man.
The sun works in my veins like wine, like wine!
'Tis a fair world: if dark, indeed, with woe,
Yet having hope and hint of such a joy,
That a man, winning, well might turn aside,   120
Careless of Heaven . . .
           O enough; I turn
From the sun's light, or haply I shall hope.
I have hoped enough; I would not hope again:
'Tis hope that is most cruel.
            Tom, my friend,
You very sorry philosophic fool;
'Tis you, I think, that bid me be resigned,
Trust, and be thankful.
          Out on you! Resigned?
I'm not resigned, not patient, not schooled in
To take my starveling's portion and pretend
I'm grateful for it. I want all, all, all;   130
I've appetite for all. I want the best:
Love, beauty, sunlight, nameless joy of life.
There's too much patience in the world I think.
We have grown base with crooking of the knee.
Mankind—say—God has bidden to a feast;
The board is spread, and groans with cates and drinks;
In troop the guests; each man with appetite
Keen-whetted with expectance.
           In they troop,
Struggle for seats, jostle and push and seize.
What's this? what's this? There are not seats for all!   140
Some men must stand without the gates; and some
Must linger by the table, ill-supplied

With broken meats. One man gets meat for two,
The while another hungers. If I stand
Without the portals, seeing others eat
Where I had thought to satiate the pangs
Of mine own hunger; shall I then come forth
When all is done, and drink my Lord's good health
In my Lord's water? Shall I not rather turn
And curse him, curse him for a niggard host?   150
O, I have hungered, hungered, through the years,
Till appetite grows craving, then disease;
I am starved, withered, shrivelled.
                                        Peace, O peace!
This rage is idle; what avails to curse
The nameless forces, the vast silences
That work in all things.
                            This time is the third,
I wrought before in heat, stung mad with pain,
Blind, scarcely understanding; now I know
What thing I do.
                    There was a woman once;
Deep eyes she had, white hands, a subtle smile,   160
Soft speaking tones: she did not break my heart,
Yet haply had her heart been otherwise
Mine had not now been broken. Yet, who knows?
My life was jarring discord from the first:
Tho' here and there brief hints of melody,
Of melody unutterable, clove the air.
From this bleak world, into the heart of night,
The dim, deep bosom of the universe,
I cast myself. I only crave for rest;
Too heavy is the load. I fling it down.   170

Epilogue

We knocked and knocked; at last, burst in the door,
And found him as you know—the outstretched arms
Propping the hidden face. The sun had set,
And all the place was dim with lurking shade.
There was no written word to say farewell,
Or make more clear the deed.
                                I searched and searched;
The room held little: just a row of books

Much scrawled and noted; sketches on the wall,
Done rough in charcoal; the old instrument
(A violin, no Stradivarius)   180
He played so ill on; in the table drawer
Large schemes of undone work. Poems half-writ;
Wild drafts of symphonies; big plans of fugues;
Some scraps of writing in a woman's hand:
No more—the scattered pages of a tale,
A sorry tale that no man cared to read.
Alas, my friend, I loved him well, tho' he
Held me a cold and stagnant-blooded fool,
Because I am content to watch, and wait
With a calm mind the issue of all things.   190
Certain it is my blood's no turbid stream;
Yet, for all that, haply I understood
More than he ever deemed; nor held so light
The poet in him. Nay, I sometimes doubt
If they have not, indeed the better part—
These poets who get drunk with sun, and weep
Because the night or a woman's face is fair.
Meantime there is much talk about my friend.
The women say, of course, he died for love;
The men, for lack of gold, or cavilling   200
Of carping critics. I, Tom Leigh, his friend.
I have no word at all to say of this.
Nay, I had deemed him more philosopher:
For did he think by this one paltry deed
To cut the knot of circumstance, and snap
The chain which binds all being?

1884

Ballade of an Omnibus

Some men to carriages aspire;
On some the costly hansoms wait;
Some seek a fly, on job or hire;
Some mount the trotting steed, elate.
I envy not the rich and great,

A wandering minstrel, poor and free,
I am contented with my fate—
An omnibus suffices me.

In winter days of rain and mire
I find within a corner strait;   10
The 'busmen know me and my lyre
From Brompton to the Bull-and-Gate.
When summer comes, I mount in state
The topmost summit, whence I see
Croesus* look up, compassionate—
An omnibus suffices me.

I mark, untroubled by desire,
Lucullus'* phaeton and its freight.
The scene whereof I cannot tire,
The human tale of love and hate,   20
The city pageant, early and late
Unfolds itself, rolls by, to be
A pleasure deep and delicate.
An omnibus suffices me.

Princess, your splendour you require,
I, my simplicity; agree
Neither to rate lower nor higher.
An omnibus suffices me.

                                        1889

Youth and Love

What does youth know of love?
    Little enough, I trow!
He plucks the myrtle for his brow,
    For his forehead the rose.
        Nay, but of love
    It is not youth who knows.

                                        1889

Contradictions

Now, even, I cannot think it true,
My friend, that there is no more you.
Almost as soon were no more I,
Which were, of course, absurdity!
Your place is bare, you are not seen,
Your grave, I'm told, is growing green;
And both for you and me, you know,
There's no Above and no Below.
That you are dead must be inferred,
And yet my thought rejects the word.   10

1889

In September

The sky is silver-grey; the long
   Slow waves caress the shore.—
On such a day as this I have been glad,
   Who shall be glad no more.

1889

JEAN INGELOW

Loss and Waste

Up to far Osteroe and Suderoe,*
  The deep sea floor lies strewn with Spanish wrecks,
O'er minted gold the fair-haired fishers go,
  O'er sunken bravery of high carved decks.

In earlier days great Carthage* suffered bale
  (All her waste works choke under sandy shoals);
And reckless hands tore down the temple veil;
  And Omar burned the Alexandrian rolls.*

The Old World arts men suffered not to last,
  Flung down they trampled lie and sunk from view,
He lets wild forest for these ages past
  Grow over the lost cities of the New.

O for a life that shall not be refused
To see the lost things found, and waste things used.

1885

Compensation

One launched a ship, but she was wrecked at sea;
  He built a bridge, but floods have borne it down;
He meant much good, none came: strange destiny,
  His corn lies sunk, his bridge bears none to town,
  Yet good he had not meant became his crown;
For once at work, when even as nature free,
  From thought of good he was, or of renown,
God took the work for good and let good be.

So wakened with a trembling after sleep,
  Dread Mona Roa* yields her fateful store;   10
All gleaming hot the scarlet rivers creep,
  And fanned of great-leaved palms slip to the shore,
Then stolen to unplumbed wastes of that far deep,
  Lay the foundations for one island more.

                                                    1886

AGNES MARY ROBINSON

Darwinism

When first the unflowering Fern-forest
  Shadowed the dim lagoons of old,
A vague unconscious long unrest
  Swayed the great fronds of green and gold.

Until the flexible stem grew rude,
  The fronds began to branch and bower,
And lo! upon the unblossoming wood
  There breaks a dawn of apple-flower.

Then on the fruitful Forest-boughs
  For ages long the unquiet ape   10
Swung happy in his airy house
  And plucked the apple and sucked the grape.

Until in him at length there stirred
  The old, unchanged, remote distress,
That pierced his world of wind and bird
  With some divine unhappiness.

Not Love, nor the wild fruits he sought;
  Nor the fierce battles of his clan
Could still the unborn and aching thought
  Until the brute became the man.   20

Long since . . . And now the same unrest
  Goads to the same invisible goal,
Till some new gift, undreamed, unguessed
  End the new travail of the soul.

1888

*Selva Oscura**

In a wood
  Far away,
Thrushes brood,
  Ravens prey,
Eagles circle overhead,
Through the boughs a bird drops dead.

Wild and high,
  The angry wind
Wanders by
  And cannot find
Any limit to the wood
Full of cries and solitude.

1893

MARGARET L. WOODS

The Sowers

Woe to the seed
　The winds carry
O'er fallow and mead!
　They do not tarry.

They seek the sea,
　The barren strand,
Where foam-flakes flee
　O'er the salt land.

Where the sharp spray
　And sand are blown,　　　　　10
In the wind's play
　The seed is sown.

Falling on shore
　It cries, 'The earth
Opens her door!
　There shall be birth

From thee far place
　From thee fair hour,
Splendour and grace
　Of leaf and flower.'　　　　　20

Falling on sea
　It cries, 'Again
Com'st thou to me,
　Refreshing rain—

Only more great,
　More strong thou art
Like to my fate,
　Like to my heart.'

On barren shore,
  Or sullen wave,   30
When storms are o'er
  It finds a grave.

1889

DORA GREENWELL

Fidelity Rewarded

'We experimented on dogs—old,
and otherwise useless'
PROFESSOR RUTHERFORD

I was not useful? So
  He says, nor young nor strong.
My master ought to know,
  I've followed him so long.

For many and many a day
  I followed well content,
Might I but go the way
  That he, my master, went.

I listened for his foot,
  I strove his thought to scan;   10
For I was but a brute,
  And he I loved was man.

O'er all that he held dear,
  A patient watch to keep,
With light, attentive ear
  I listened in my sleep.

The stealthy foot withdrew,
  The daring hand was stayed;
My growl the robber knew,
  And fled the spot dismayed.   20

I knew my master's voice,
  My nature's bounded plan
Had left my love no choice,
  And he I loved was man.

And often would I watch
  His inmost thought to prove,
His hidden will to catch:
  A brute can only love.

I waited for a crumb,
  From off his daily meal 30
To fall for me: a dumb
  Poor brute can only feel.

I thought he loved me well,
  But when my eye grew dim—
I leave the tale to tell
  As it is told by him—

Some secret hint to track
  Of life's poor trembling flame,
He nailed me to a rack,
  He pierced and tore my frame. 40

He saw me slowly die
  In agonies acute:
For he was man, and I
  Was nothing but a brute!

1889

Only a Smile

No butterfly whose frugal fare
  Is breath of heliotrope and clove,
And other trifles light as air,
  Could live on less than doth my love.

That childlike smile that comes and goes
  About your gracious lips and eyes,
Hath all the sweetness of the rose,
  Which feeds the freckled butterflies.

I feed my love on smiles, and yet
  Sometimes I ask, with tears of woe,   10
How had it been if we had met,
  If you had met me long ago,

Before the fast, defacing years
  Had made all ill that once was well?
Ah, then your smiling breeds such tears
  As Tantalus* may weep in hell.

1893

Across a Gaudy Room

Across a gaudy room
I looked and saw his face,
Beneath the sapless palm-trees, in the gloom
Of the distressing place,
Where everyone sat tired,
Where talk itself grew stale,
Where, as the day began to fail,
No guest had just the power required
To rise and go: I strove with my disgust;
But at the sight of him my eyes were fired   10
To give one glance, as though they must
Be sociable with what they found of fair
And free and simple in a chamber where
Life was so base.

As when a star is lit
In the dull evening sky,
Another soon leaps out to answer it,
Even so the bright reply
Came sudden from his eyes,
By all but me unseen;   20
Since then the distance that between
Our lives unalterably lies
Is but a darkness, intimate and still,
Which messages may traverse, where replies
May sparkle from afar, until
The night becomes a mystery made clear
Between two souls forbidden to draw near:
Creator, why?

1893

Second Thoughts

I thought of leaving her for a day
In town, it was such an iron winter
At Durdans, the garden frosty clay,
The woods as dry as any splinter,
The sky congested. I would break
From the deep, lethargic, country air
To the shining lamps, to the clash of the play,
And, tomorrow, wake
Beside her, a thousand things to say.
I planned—O more—I had almost started;   10
I lifted her face in my hands to kiss,
A face in a border of fox's fur,
For the bitter black wind had stricken her,
And she wore it—her soft hair straying out
Where it buttoned against the gray, leather snout:
In an instant we should have parted;
But at sight of the delicate world within
That fox-fur collar, from brow to chin,
At sight of those wonderful eyes from the mine,
Coal pupils, an iris of glittering spa,   20
And the wild, ironic, defiant shine
As of a creature behind a bar
One has captured, and, when three lives are past,
May hope to reach the heart of at last,
All that, and the love at her lips, combined
To show me what folly it were to miss
A face with such thousand things to say,
And beside these, such thousand more to spare,
For the shining lamps, for the clash of the play—
O madness; not for a single day   30
Could I leave her! I stayed behind

                                        undated

MAY KENDALL

In the Drawing-Room

Furniture with the languid mien,
  On which life seems to pall—
With your insipid grey and green
  And drab, your cheerless wall—
To think that she has really been
  An hour among you all.

I wonder, since she went away,
  Has no one ever guessed
Why constantly you look more grey,
  More green, and more depressed.
I know—you know, you had your day,
  Now you need only rest.

You heavy, yellow easy-chair,
  Right opposite the door,
Ah, how impassively you stare
  Across the dreary floor;
Yet even you would be aware
  If she should come once more.

I see the dingy curtains stir
  With a faint memory;
The grand piano dreams of her
  In a drowsy minor key.
Rest tranquilly, old furniture,
  Tonight it may not be!

1894

DOLLIE RADFORD

From Our Emancipated Aunt in Town

All has befallen as I say,
The old regime has passed away,
   And quite a new one

Is being fashioned in a fire,
The fervours of whose burning tire
   And quite undo one.

The fairy prince has passed from sight,
Away into the ewigkeit,*
   With best intention

I served him, as you know my dreams,   10
Unfalteringly through more years
   Than ladies mention.

And though the fairy prince has gone,
With all the props I leaned upon,
   And I am stranded,

With old ideals blown away,
And all opinions, in the fray,
   Long since disbanded.

And though he's only left to me,
Of course quite inadvertently,   20
   The faintest glimmer

Of humour, to illume my way,
I'm thankful he has had his day,
   His shine and shimmer.

Le roi est mort—but what's to come?—
Surcharged the air is with the hum
   Of startling changes

And our great 'question' is per force
The vital one, o'er what a course
   It boldly ranges!   30

Strange gentlemen to me express
At quiet 'at homes' their willingness,
   To ease our fetters

And ladies, in a fleeting car,
Will tell me that the moderns are
   My moral betters.

My knees I know are much too weak
To mount the high and shady peak
   Of latest ethics

I'm tabulated, and I stand   40
By evolution, in a band
   Of poor pathetics

Who cannot go alone, who cling
To many a worn out tottering thing
   Of a convention;

To many a prejudice and hope,
And to the old proverbial rope
   Of long dimension.

It is to you to whom I look
To beautify our history book,   50
   For coming readers,

To you my nieces, who must face
Our right and wrong, and take your place
   As future leaders.

And I, meanwhile, shall still pursue
All that is weird and wild and new,
   In song and ballet,

In lecture, drama, verse and prose,
With every cult that comes and goes
   Your aunt will dally.   60

A microscopic analyst
Of female hearts, she will subsist
   On queerest notions

And subtlest views of maid and wife
Ever engaged in deadly strife
With the emotions.

But while you walk, and smile at her,
In quiet lanes which you prefer
   To public meetings,

Remember she prepares your way,   70
With many another Aunt today,
   And send her greetings.

1895

Mother and Daughter

16

She will not have it that my day wanes low,
  Poor of the fire its drooping sun denies,
  That on my brow the thin lines write goodbyes
Which soon may be read plain for all to know,
Telling that I have done with youth's brave show;
  Alas! and done with youth in heart and eyes,
  With wonder and with far expectancies,
Save but to say 'I knew such long ago.'

She will not have it. Loverlike to me,
  She with her happy gaze finds all that's best,   10
She sees this fair and that unfretted still,
  And her own sunshine over all the rest:
So she half keeps me as she'd have me be,
And I forget to age, through her sweet will.

24

'You scarcely are a mother, at that rate.
  Only one child!' The blithe soul pitied loud.
  And doubtless she, amid her household crowd,
When one brings care in another's fortunate;
When one fares forth another's at her gate.
  Yea were her first-born folded in his shroud,
  Not with a whole despair would she be bowed,
She has more sons to make her heart elate.

Many to love her singly, mother theirs,
  To give her the dear love of being their need,   10
  To storm her lap by turns and claim their kiss,
To kneel around her at their bed-time prayers;
  Many to grow her comrades! Some have this.
  Yet I, I do not envy them indeed.

25

You think that you love each as much as one,
  Mothers with many nestlings 'neath your wings.
  Nay, but you know not. Love's most priceless things
Have unity that cannot be undone.
You give the rays, I the englobed full sun;
  I give the river, you the separate springs:
  My motherhood's all my child's with all it brings—
None takes the strong entireness from her: none.

You know not. You love yours with various stress;
  This with a graver trust, this with more pride;   10
  This maybe with more needed tenderness:
I by each uttermost passion of my soul
Am turned to mine; she is one, she has the whole:
  How should you know who appraise love and divide.

27

Since first my little one lay on my breast
  I never needed such a second good,
  Nor felt a void left in my motherhood
She filled not always to the utterest.
The summer linnet, by glad yearnings pressed,
  Builds room enough to house a callow brood:
  I prayed not for another child—nor could;
My solitary bird had my heart's nest.

But she is cause that any baby thing
  If it but smile, is one of mine in truth,   10
  And every child becomes my natural joy:
And, if my heart gives all youth fostering,
  Her sister, brother, seems the girl or boy:
My darling makes me mother to their youth.

1895

Slowly

Heavy is my heart,
Dark are thine eyes.
Thou and I must part
Ere the sun rise.

Ere the sun rise,
Thou and I must part.
Dark are thine eyes,
Heavy my heart.

1896

Gone

About the little chambers of my heart
Friends have been coming—going—many a year.
  The doors stand open there.
Some, lightly stepping, enter; some depart.

Freely they come and freely go, at will
The walls give back their laughter; all day long
  They fill the house with song.
One door alone is shut, one chamber still.

1896

The Other Side of the Mirror

I sat before my glass one day,
And conjured up a vision bare,
Unlike the aspects glad and gay,
That erst was found reflected there—
The vision of a woman, wild
With more than womanly despair.

Her hair stood back on either side
A face bereft of loveliness.
It had no envy now to hide
What once no man on earth could guess.   10
It formed the thorny aureole
Of hard, unsanctified distress.

Her lips were open—not a sound
Came through the parted lines of red,
Whate'er it was, the hideous wound
In silence and in secret bled.
No sigh relieved her speechless woe,
She had no voice to speak her dread.

And in her lurid eyes there shone
The dying flames of life's desire,   20
Made mad because its hope was gone,
And kindled at the leaping fire
Of jealousy and fierce revenge,
And strength that could not change nor tire.

Shade of a shadow in the glass,
O set the crystal surface free!
Pass—as the fairer visions pass—
Nor ever more return, to be
The ghost of a distracted hour,
That heard me whisper: 'I am she!'   30

1896

An Anniversary

Three years! Is it only three?
A weary while has passed since then.
The world of nature and of men
Is older, by an age, to me.

Three years! And is it then so long?
I thought it happened yesterday.
How is it with thee, far away,
In the white world of palm and song?

1896

Not Yet

Time brought me many another friend
    That loved me longer.
New love was kind, but in the end
    Old love was stronger.

Years come and go. No New Year yet
    Hath slain December.
And all that should have cried—'Forget!'
    Cries but—'Remember!'

1896

He Knoweth that the Dead Are Thine

The weapon that you fought with was a word,
And with that word you stabbed me to the heart.
Not once but twice you did it, for the sword
    Made no blood start.

They have not tried you for your life. You go
Strong in such innocence as men will boast.
They have not buried me. They do not know
　Life from its ghost.

1896

At Dead of Night

There was not a moon, but half a moon,
And the stars were faint and few.
There were clouds full soon at the night's high noon,
And a rollicking wind that blew.

There were three that bled, there was one that led,
Where they fought with four and three.
The silvery swords were crimson red,
And the grass was a sight to see.

They laughed as they fell, and they died right well,
And they called to their foes for more.   10
'We will go to Hell, but the tale we'll tell
Of the seven that fought with four!'

1896

I Ask of Thee

I ask of thee, love, nothing but relief.
Thou canst not bring the old days back again;
For I was happy then,
Not knowing heavenly joy, not knowing grief.

1897

L'Oiseau Bleu

The lake lay blue below the hill.
O'er it, as I looked there flew
Across the waters, cold and still,
A bird whose wings were palest blue.

The sky above was blue at last,
The sky beneath me blue in blue.
A moment, ere the bird had passed,
It caught his image as he flew.

1897

DORA SIGERSON

My Neighbour's Garden

Why in my neighbour's garden
Are the flowers more sweet than mine?
I never had such bloom of roses,
Such yellow and pink woodbine.

Why in my neighbour's garden
Are the fruits all red and gold,
While here the grapes are bitter
That hang for my fingers' hold?

Why in my neighbour's garden
Do the birds all fly to sing?   10
Over the fence between us
One would think 'twas always spring.

I thought my own wide garden
Once more sweet and fair than all,
Till I saw the gold and crimson
Just over my neighbour's wall.

But now I want his thrushes,
And now I want his vine,
If I cannot have his cherries
That grow more red than mine.   20

The serpent 'neath his apples
Will tempt me to my fall,
And then—I'll steal my neighbour's fruit
Across the garden wall.

1898

Beware

I closed my hands upon a moth
  And when I drew my palms apart,
Instead of dusty broken wings
  I found a bleeding heart.

I crushed my foot upon a worm
  That had my garden for its goal,
But when I drew my foot aside
  I found a dying human soul.

1898

At Pompeii

At Pompeii I heard a woman laugh,
And turned to find the reason of her mirth,
Saw but the silent figure of a girl
That centuries had mummied into earth:

The running figure of a little maid
With face half-hidden in her shielding arm,
Silent, yet screaming, yea in every limb,
The cruel torture of her dread alarm.

At Pompeii I heard a maiden shriek
All down the years from out the distant past;   10
Blind in the awful darkness still she runs;
Death in the mould of fear her form has cast.

A little maid once soft and sweet and white,
Full of the morning's hope, and love and joy,
That Nature, moving to the voice of Time,
Shook her dark wings to wither and destroy.

At Pompeii I saw a woman bend
Above this dead, pronounce an epitaph;
The mother of a child, it may have been.
Oh horrible! I heard a woman laugh.

1899

MOIRA O'NEILL

*Sea Wrack**

The wrack was dark an' shiny where it floated in the sea,
There was no one in the brown boat but only him an' me;
Him to cut the sea wrack, me to mind the boat,
An' not a word between us the hours we were afloat.
   The wet wrack,
   The sea wrack,
   The wrack was strong to cut.

We laid it on the grey rocks to wither in the sun,
An' what should call my lad then, to sail from Cushendun?
With a low moon, a full tide, a swell upon the deep   10
Him to sail the old boat, me to fall asleep.
   The dry wrack,
   The sea wrack,
   The wrack was dead so soon.

There's a fire low upon the rocks to burn the wrack to kelp,
There's a boat gone down upon the Moyle, an' sorra* one to
    help!
Him beneath the salt sea, me upon the shore,
By sunlight or moonlight we'll lift the wrack no more.
   The dark wrack,
   The sea wrack,   20
   The wrack may drift ashore.

1900

The Grand Match

Dennis was hearty when Dennis was young,
High was his step in the jig that he sprung,
He had the looks an' the sootherin' tongue,—
    An' he wanted a girl wid a fortune.

Nannie was grey-eyed an' Nannie was tall,
Fair was the face hidin' under her shawl,
Troth! an' he liked her the best o' them all,—
    But she'd not a *traneen* to her fortune.

He be to look out for a likelier match,
So he married a girl that was counted a catch,   10
An' as ugly as need be, the dark little patch,—
    But that was a thrifle,* he tould her.

She brought him her good-lookin' gold to admire,
She brought him her good-lookin' cows to his byre,
But far from good-lookin' she sat by his fire.—
    An' paid him that 'thrifle' he tould her.

He met pretty Nan when a month had gone by,
An' he thought like a fool to get round her he'd try;
Wid a smile on her lip an' a spark in her eye,
    She said, 'How is the woman that owns ye?'   20

Och, never be tellin' the life that he's led!
Sure many's the night that he'll wish himself dead,
For the sake o' two eyes in a pretty girl's head,—
    An' the tongue o' the woman that owns him.

                                        1900

NOTES

_____

p. 8 **Jane:** Tom Winnifrith suggests that 'Jane' is Charlotte herself (*The Poems of Charlotte Brontë*, 1984, p. 351), but her two sisters, Maria and Elizabeth, had died in 1824, and thus this elegiac poem might refer to a 'presentiment' in the past.

p. 15 **'The North Wind':** this poem is purportedly written from prison by 'Alexandrina Zenobia', one of the characters that Anne and Emily Brontë constructed for the fictional world of Gondal (see Note on Anne Brontë, p. xi).

p. 16 **Thorp Green:** Anne Brontë was governess to the two daughters of the Rev. Edmund Robinson at Thorp Green, in the parish of Little Ouseburn, Yorkshire, from early in the year 1841 until June 1845.

p. 17 **'Appeal':** the original title was 'Lines written at Thorp Green'.

p. 20 **'Domestic Peace':** this poem was written during the time that the brother of the Brontë sisters, Patrick Branwell Brontë, was disturbing the home at Haworth Parsonage by his drunken intemperance and 'frantic folly' in relation to his former employer's wife.

p. 25 **'Faith and Despondency':** this dialogue between Ierne and her father arose from the Gondal stories.

p. 27 **'Remembrance':** a slightly earlier draft of this poem has no title, but is headed, 'R[osina] Alcons to J[ulius] Brenzaida', which shows that the poem once formed part of the Gondal cycle (see Note on Anne Brontë, p. xi).

p. 27 **fifteen wild Decembers:** this is a reference to chronology in the Gondal stories which exist only in fragments.

p. 39 **Sonnets from the Portuguese:** these eight sonnets are part of a series which celebrate the love between Elizabeth Barrett (1806–61) and Robert Browning (1812–89). The title, which alludes to the Portuguese poet, Luis de Camoens (1524–80), represents Barrett Browning's attempt to disguise the autobiographical content of these sonnets.

p. 39 Theocritus: (*c.* 300–260 BC) a Greek pastoral poet, was noted for trying new forms, or using old forms in new ways. Barrett Browning's sonnets are regularly Petrarchan, but new in subject matter in that they are in the voice of a woman poet.

p. 40 Electra: Electra, in Greek mythology, encouraged her brother Orestes to murder Clytemnestra, her mother, after her mother had murdered her husband and Electra's beloved father, Agamemnon. Barrett Browning implies that her love for her own father is in ashes.

p. 41 Rialto: the Rialto, which is at the centre of mercantile old Venice, is a marble bridge across the Grand Canal. Barrett Browning suggests that the soul has spiritual merchandise.

p. 41 Pindar: Pindar (518–438 BC) was a Greek lyric poet, who celebrated the nine Muses—the female gods who presided over the arts, including poetry. Barrett Browning is indirectly comparing Robert Browning to the Muses and herself to Pindar.

p. 42 Aurora Leigh: the passages used are excerpts from the first of nine books of this verse novel, of which a major theme is its record of the growth of a poet's sensibility. Although this poem thus echoes Wordsworth's *The Prelude* (1820, rev. 1850) in part, her conception of plotting a novel in blank verse is original.

p. 43 Love's Divine: Exodus 3:2, a mother's love is compared to Divine Love.

p. 46 Psyche: Psyche, in the allegorical tale of Apuleius, loses the love of Cupid because she does not trust him.

p. 46 Medusa: in Greek legend, Medusa was one of the three female Gorgons, of hideous appearance, winged, their heads wreathed with serpents instead of hair, with the power of turning to stone those who looked directly at them. Medusa was beheaded by Perseus through the trick of looking at her in a burnished shield.

p. 46 Our Lady of the Passion: this refers to the Virgin Mary who, in Christian mythology, suffered the death of her Son, Jesus Christ.

p. 46 Lamia: *see* John Keats, *Lamia* (1820).

p. 52 Tracts against the times: Newman's *Tracts for the Times* are ironically against reform.

p. 52 Buonaventure: Saint Buonaventure (1221–74) was a supporter of love and not logical reasoning.

p. 54 **Brinvilliers**: Marie Brinvilliers (c. 1630–76), a murderess, was tortured by being made to drink an excessive amount of water, an event which the poet compares to her education.

p. 56 **Ganymede**: Ganymede, a youth of Phrygia, Greece, was commanded by the god, Zeus, to become cup-bearer to the gods in place of Hebe.

p. 59 **Muse-Sphinx**: an ironic reference to P. B. Shelley's poem, 'Ozymandias'.

p. 80 **Ruth**: in the Book of Ruth, ii–iv, after the death of her husband, Ruth returns with her mother-in-law, Naomi, to her mother-in-law's kinsfolk. She gleans wheat and corn for Boaz, a kinsman of hers by marriage. Her reward for this work is marriage with him, but Naomi is given her baby from this union.

p. 82 '*Qui primavera sempre ed ogni frutto*': '*Here always spring and every fruit.*'

p. 82 '*Ragionando con meco ed io con lui*': '*Conversing with me and I with him.*'

p. 82 'love is strong as death': The Song of Solomon, 8:6.

p. 83 '*Con miglior corso e con migliore stella*': 'With better course and with better stars.'

p. 83 '*La vita fugge e non s'arresta un' ora*': 'Life flees and stays not an hour.'

p. 83 '*Vien dietro a me e lascia dir le genti*': 'Come after me, and leave folk to talk.'

p. 83 '*Contando i easi della vita nostra*': 'Relating the casualties of our life.'

p. 84 '*Amor che ne la mentemi ragiona*': 'Love, who speaks within my mind.'

p. 84 '*Amor vien nel bel viso di costei*': 'Love comes in the beautiful face of this lady.'

p. 84 '*E la Sua Volontade è nostra pace*': 'And His will is our peace.'

p. 84 '*Sol con questi pensier, con altre chiome*': 'Only with these thoughts, with different locks.'

p. 89 Glossary of terms: *afiel*, from home; *douce*, gentle; *farrant*, sagacious; *chiel*, fellow, man; *crack*, gossip; *pack*, friendly; *pree*, experience, pry; *gumption*, quickness of understanding, independence of spirit; *lang-nebbit*, pedantic; *wrocht*, struggled with, wrought; *whilk*, which; *stacher*, stagger; *stoit*, stumble; *tummle*, tumble; *glunch*, frown; *grumil*, grumble; *delvit*, working hard, delving; *dungit*, nudging; *yird*, earth; *loosit*, loosened; *labourit*, laboured over; *leuk*, look; *crap*, crop; *streekin'*, stretching; *neives*, fists; *jaukin'*, joking; *ahin*, behind in time; *yirth*, earth; *taes*, fork prongs; *ugsume*, disgusting, ugly; *mense*, good manners; *ill deedie*, mischievous; *taes*, toes; *lear*, learning; *snod*, tidy; *eident*, industrious; *thrang*, absorbing; *leal*, loyal; *fyke*, fuss; *shooster lassies*, semptresses; *teeps*, types; *herry*, to rob nests, to harry; *aiblins*, possibly; *ilk*, each; *coosten*, cast; *thole*, to suffer; *ware*, to expend.

p. 91 Bessie Park: Bessie Park (1829–1925), an advocate of the rights of women to education for and employment in the professions, wrote *Remarks on the Education of Girls* (1854), and published (with Barbara Bodichon) *The Englishwoman's Journal* with the aim of stimulating women's interest in entering the professions.

p. 93 'Brother and Sister': this series of eleven sonnets refers to George Eliot's early years with her brother, Isaac (see Notes on the Authors p. xv).

p. 100 Glossary of terms: *sweir*, reluctant; *thrang*, absorbed; *waefu*, woeful; *pickle siller*, small quantity of money; *lease me o*, an expression of extreme affection for; *tow*, flax; *puirtith*, poverty; *mickle*, much.

p. 105 *Vies Manquées*: failed lives.

p. 113 Laplace: Pierre Laplace (1745–1827) was a French mathematician and astronomer.

p. 113 Herbert Spencer: (1820–1903), an English evolutionary philosopher, he postulated the theory of evolution prior to Charles Darwin's *The Descent of Man*.

p. 114 *Aves*: birds.

p. 114 *Homo*: human being.

p. 118 *Hamlet*, III, i.

p. 119 Sisyphus: one of the damned who is tormented in Hades.

p. 120 Theocritus: see note, p. 153.

p. 120 Prometheus' bard: Hesiod (*c.* 700 BC), a well-known Greek poet.

p. 124 Croesus: (*c.* 560–46 BC) was reputedly wealthy.

p. 124 Lucullus: (*c.* 110–57 BC) acquired prodigious wealth and spent his money on luxuries.

p. 126 Osteroe and Suderoe: two of the Faeroe Islands, which are now part of Denmark.

p. 126 Carthage: at one time at war with Rome, it was completely destroyed in *c.* 146 BC.

p. 126 And Omar burned the Alexandrian rolls: the Caliph Omar (*c.* 581–64 BC) is said to have burned the manuscript library at Alexandria.

p. 127 Mona Roa: a volcano in Hawaii (now Mauna Loa).

p. 129 'Selva Oscura': *Selva* is a 'tract of densely wooded country lying in the basin of the River Amazon' (*OED*); *oscura* is Spanish for 'dark', or, figuratively speaking, 'unenlightened' (*OED*).

p. 134 Tantalus: in Greek mythology, Tantalus abused the privileges he had been granted and, because he was immortal, he was afflicted with eternal punishment.

p. 138 ewigkeit: eternity.

p. 151 wrack: sea weed.

p. 151 sorra: sorry that.

p. 152 thrifle: a small amount of money.

CRITICAL RESPONSES

This extract from Edmund Gosse's 1882 essay on Christina Rossetti's poetry is a representative example of the kind of dismissive judgments that were made about Victorian women poets towards the end of the era in which they wrote.

Woman, for some reason which seems to have escaped the philosopher, has never taken a very prominent position in the history of poetry. But she has rarely been absent altogether from any great revival of poetic literature. The example of her total absence which immediately flies to the recollection is the most curious of all. That Shakespeare should have had no female rival, that the age in which music burdened every bough, and in which poets made their appearance in hundreds, should have produced not a solitary authentic poetess, even of the fifth rank, this is curious indeed. But it is rare as it is curious, for though women have not taken a very high position on Parnassus, they have seldom thus wholly absented themselves . . .

It is no new theory that women, in order to succeed in poetry, must be brief, personal and concentrated . . . At no time is it more necessary to insist on this truth than it is today. The multiplication of books of verse, the hackneyed character of all obvious notation of life and feeling, should, one would fancy, tend to make our poets more exiguous, more concise, more trimly girt. There are few men now for whom the immense flood of writing can be endured without fatigue; few who can hold the trumpet to their lips for hours in the market-place without making a desert around them. Yet there never was a time when the pouring out of verse was less restrained. Everything that occurs to the poet seems, today, to be worth writing down and printing. The result is the neglect of really good and charming work, which misses all effect because it is drowned in stuff that is second- or third-rate. The women who write, in particular, pursued by that commercial fervour which is so curious a feature of our new literary life, and which sits so inelegantly upon a female figure, are in a ceaseless hurry to work off and hurry away into oblivion those qualities of their style which might, if seriously and coyly guarded, attract a permanent attention ('Christina Rossetti' in *Critical Kit-Kats*, 1896, reprinted in *The Victorian Poet*, edited by Joseph Bristow, pp. 138–9).

Ifor Evans, the literary historian, is one of the few early twentieth-century critics who essayed aesthetic judgments about a few Victorian women writers other than the 'big two'— Elizabeth Barrett Browning and Christina Rossetti.

Among the minor poets of the later nineteenth century are some women writers. Their work is difficult to classify, and on its value the most divergent judgments have been passed. The clearest tradition is that maintained by the popular women poets, the writers of lyric, of facile movement, and of simple, sometimes mawkish sentiment. Even the greater women writers—Mrs Browning and Christina Rossetti—descend at times to this level. Adelaide Anne Procter (1825–64) is an example of this popular tradition in the earlier part of the century. She was a *Household Words* poet and wrote sometimes the verse that Dickens's heroines might have enjoyed. She can do much better, as *A Legend of Provence* issued in *Legends and Lyrics* (1858–61) shows. Jean Ingelow (1820–97), a poet and a novelist, suffered from the same defects, yet she possessed a more definite lyrical quality. Her verse, *Poems* (1863), *A Story of Doom* (1867), and *Poems* (1885), gained a wide audience, and encouraged her innate prolixity. She attempted some ambitious things, but she approaches poetry only in simple ballad and lyric, in 'The High Tide on the Coast of Lincolnshire, 1571', and in 'Divided'. Even here she has an overflow of words, and unremitting sweetness in melody reminiscent of some of Tennyson's early lyrics.

In contrast with these practitioners of fluid verse may be found a few writers whose output is small and who have obviously exercised self-criticism. The published work of Margaret Veley (1843–87) is in such a small compass that probably she would have remained unknown had not Leslie Stephen introduced some of her poems into the *Cornhill* and later prepared an edition of her verses, *A Marriage of Shadows* (1888). Even when assembled, her verses seem a slender collection of shy pieces content to be forgotten. She possessed a classical quality in verse, precision without a thrusting for unusual effects, and an economy in vocabulary reminiscent of Robert Bridges. Her best-remembered poem, 'A Japanese Fan', a delicate study in irony and sentiment, shows a lover using the legend on a fan to relate how his mistress ill-used him … Into her other verses melancholy occasionally intrudes, and she returns to the 'When I am dead' mood of

Christina Rossetti; but her more individual talent lay in description, which she shows in such poems as 'Sunset', 'The Land of Shadows', and 'A Town Garden'. She can erect a mood out of a mosaic of detail, and there remains from her poetry an image of twilit waters, bridges, and laden ships, and roads 'dim and ashengray'. These nocturnes are executed without any lavish expenditure of verbal resources, and this act of self-denial in style separates her from many of the other women writers of her time, and shows that small as her output may be she possessed the intuitions and the methods of a poet.

Some have found equal strength in the work of Amy Levy (1861–89), a novelist and poet whose talent was undoubtedly developing when she brought her own life to an end in 1889. Her poetry is contained in three volumes, *Xantippe* (1881), *A Minor Poet* (1884), and *A London Plane-Tree* (1889). In lyric she develops a movement of song on whose somewhat facile melodies the influence of Heine can be traced; but in her last volume, *A London Plane-Tree*, she shows a greater restraint and a capacity for converting significant experiences into compact lyrics. Her two most telling poems are, however, in blank verse. 'A Minor Poet' is a study of suicide, reminiscent of Browning's methods, but fresh and independent enough, nor does its whole strength derive from the premonition it contains of her own fate. *Xantippe*, a study of Socrates' wife, has an originality derived from its exposition of a woman's point of view, but the verse is modelled too closely on Browning. Amy Levy has a capacity in verse which is at best unfinished, but the absence of lushness and crudity suggest that she might have grown in strength. Some have discovered her most mature talent in an interesting poem on waltzing, 'Swing and Sway'.

It is difficult to discover the same authenticity in the more copious work of Mathilde Blind (1841–96), the daughter of exiles from Germany after the Revolution of 1848. A visit to Scotland led to *The Prophecy of St Oran* (1882) and *The Heath on Fire* (1886). In the first, she was captured by the romantic past, and in the second, she pleaded against the evictions of the Scottish peasantry. Her danger is to use accurate but undistinguished verse in which memories from other poets enter with irritating abruptness. More ambitious was her disastrous attempt to render poetically the century's debate on evolution in *The Ascent of Man* (1889). Her later verses, mainly lyrics and sonnets—*Dramas in Miniature* (1891), *Songs and Sonnets* (1893), *Birds of Passage* (1895)—frequently owe their suggestions to travel in Egypt and the Near East. Occasionally, she approaches towards an angle of vision which is her own, as in 'The Songs of Summer', 'The

Hunter's Moon', and 'A Fantasy'. Yet, despite the critical attention of Arthur Symons and Dr Richard Garnett, it will be found that Mathilde Blind seldom passed the gap which divides adroit versifying from poetry.

Mrs Augusta Webster (1837–94) frequently shared Mathilde Blind's pedestrian quality, but with her the pace can quicken and the verse has interest and variety. She published voluminously: *Blanche Lisle* (1860); *Lilian Gray* (1864); a translation of *Prometheus Unbound* (1866) and of *Medea* (1868); *Dramatic Studies* (1866); *A Woman Sold* (1867); *Portraits* (1870); *Yu-Pe-Ya's Lute* (1874); *A Book of Rhyme* (1884); and verse dramas, including *The Auspicious Day* (1872) and *Disguises* (1879). Mrs Webster developed under [Robert] Browning's influence, and much of her early work combines moral strenuousness with heavy blank verse. She is not a mere studio-worker: had that been her aim her work would have been easier to accomplish and might have been more lively. She had definitely a woman's attitude to express: it can be found in *A Woman Sold* (1868), and it reoccurs in *The Castaway*, a poem on the theme of a fallen woman, which gained [Robert] Browning's admiration. Her feminism gives her poetry a strength, sometimes even a corrosive quality, which distinguishes her from that of imitators and mere versifiers. Further, she can occasionally gain poetic effectiveness in handling other themes. In *The Snow Waste* (1866), she recounts a Dantesque vision of one who has sinned through jealousy, and the dread allegorical landscape around the speaker is well contrived. She showed also a spirit of experiment, as seen in her attempts in *English Stornelli* to adapt the Italian *rispetto*, an eight-line rural love lyric, into English verse. The poems are lightly turned, if occasionally a little vague and inconclusive. The same grace accompanies her 'Chinese' tale, *Yu-Pe-Ya's Lute*, where fantastic story is made pleasantly to combine with description of Chinese manners and etiquette ... *English Poets in the Later Nineteenth Century*, 1966, pp. 352–5, first published in 1933).

Kathleen Hickok is the first of contemporary literary critics to attempt a full-scale assessment of nineteenth-century British women poets, although she concentrates almost exclusively on English poets, omitting, for example, the poetry of Joanna Baillie. Moreover, in her socio-cultural methods of analysis, she discusses the content of this poetry by English women writers more than the forms that they used.

I believe we can best evaluate the representations of women by nineteenth-century women poets if we examine their work in the context of contemporary thought and in comparison with other writers' depiction of female characters. Several studies have applied this contextual approach to the images of women in the nineteenth-century novel ... But women poets of nineteenth-century England have, with only a few exceptions, received such scant attention that a great deal of poetry written by women who were significant literary figures in their day and who considered themselves to be serious artists is today virtually unknown ... the best-known today are Emily Brontë, Elizabeth Barrett Browning, and Christina Rossetti, all of whom have been accepted, albeit somewhat grudgingly, into the canon of Victorian literature. However, there were throughout the century many other women writing poetry, much of it extremely popular and highly praised in its day ...

In choosing the minor poets to consider, I was guided by both the popularity and the merit of the writer—two characteristics which were often mutually exclusive rather than complementary. Thus, the overall quality of works under consideration is unavoidably uneven. There were many volumes of mediocre poems by representative, popular women poets as well as fewer books by women who were not well known by the general public but whose poetry was of an excellent quality or was decidedly unconventional in its depiction of women ...

The inclusive approach I have adopted has several advantages. It brings these lesser-known poets to light, allowing us, for the first time in more than a hundred years in some cases, to describe and evaluate their achievements, to discover common themes and genres in their work, and to examine trends and changes in the literary history of women. Furthermore, it enables us to analyze more confidently the ways in which the better-known writers were linked with their cultural and literary peers; so that, turning in the final chapters to Elizabeth Barrett Browning and Christina Rossetti, we are better poised to evaluate their own outstanding contributions to the literary representation of women.

Although some characteristics of women's poetry in the nineteenth century can be identified as Romantic or Victorian by theme or by aesthetics, the literary history of women ultimately cannot and should not be defined solely by the literary history of men ... (*Representations of Women*, pp. 4–6).

ACKNOWLEDGEMENTS

I am grateful to R. W. Noble for his literary advice, and to Roger Sales, University of East Anglia, who kindly advised me about working-class poets. I also wish to thank the staff of the British Library, the London Library and the University of London Library at Senate House for their courteous assistance.

The editor and publisher wish to thank the following for permission to use the following material:

Blackwell Publishers for poems included in *The Poems of Charlotte Brontë*, ed. Tom Winnifrith, 1984, The Shakespeare Head Press;

Greenwood Publishing Group, Inc., for excerpts from Kathleen Hickok, *Representations of Women: Nineteenth Century British Women's Poetry*, 1984;

Skoob Books Publishing Ltd for 'In a London Drawing-Room' from George Eliot, *Collected Poems*, ed. Lucien Jenkins, 1989.

Every effort has been made to trace all the copyright holders, but if any have been inadvertently overlooked the publishers will be pleased to make the necessary arrangement at the first opportunity.

SELECT BIBLIOGRAPHY

PRIMARY WORKS

Barrett Browning, Elizabeth, *The Poetical Works*, F. G. Kenyon (ed.) (London, John Murray, 1914); *Aurora Leigh with Other Poems*, Cora Kaplan (intro.), (London, The Women's Press, 1978).

Blind, Mathilde, *Songs and Sonnets* (London, Chatto & Windus, 1893).

Brontë, Anne, *The Complete Poems*, Clement Shorter (ed.) (London, Hodder & Stoughton, 1923).

Brontë, Charlotte, *The Poems*, Tom Winnifrith (ed.) (Oxford, Shakespeare Head Press (Basil Blackwell), 1984).

Brontë, Emily Jane, *Complete Poems*, Clement Shorter (ed.) (London, Hodder & Stoughton, 1923).

The Brontës: Selected Poems, Juliet R. V. Barker (ed.) (London, Dent, 1985, 1992).

Coleridge, Mary Elizabeth, *Fancy's Following* (Oxford, Daniel Press, 1896); *Fancy's Guerdon* (London, Elkin Mathews, 1897).

Cook, Eliza, *Poems*, 2nd Series (London, Simpkin, Marshall & Co., 1845).

Eliot, George, *The Legend of Jubal and Other Poems* (London, William Blackwood & Sons, 1874); *Collected Poems*, Lucien Jenkins (ed.) (London, Skoob Books, 1989).

Field, Michael, *Long Ago* (London, George Bell & Sons, 1889); *Sight and Song* (London, Elkin Mathews and John Lane at the Bodley Head, 1892); *Underneath the Bough: A Book of Verses* (London, George Bell & Sons, 1893); *A Selection from the Poems of Michael Field*, T. E. Sturge Moore (ed.) (London; The Poetry Bookshop, 1933).

Greenwell, Dora, *Poems* (London, Walter Scott, 1889).

Howitt, Mary, *Ballads and Other Poems* (London, Longman, Brown, Green & Longmans, 1847).

Ingelow, Jean, *Poems*, 3rd Series (London, Longmans, Green & Co., 1885; *Lyrical and Other Poems* (London, Longmans, Green & Co., 1886).

Kemble, Frances Anne, *Poems* (London, Henry Washbourne, reprinted from American edition, 1844).

Kendall, May, *Dreams to Sell* (London, Longmans, Green & Co., 1887); *Songs from Dreamland* (London, Longmans, Green & Co., 1894).

Kerrigan, Catherine, *An Anthology of Scottish Poets*, Gaelic translation by Meg Bateman (Edinburgh University Press, 1991).

Levy, Amy, *A Minor Poet and other Verse* (London, T. Fisher Unwin, 1884); *A London Plane-Tree and other Verse* (London, T. Fisher Unwin, 1889).

Naden, Constance, *Songs and Sonnets of Springtime* (London, C. Kegan Paul, 1881); *A Modern Apostle; The Elixir of Life; The Story of Clarice; and Other Poems* (London, Kegan Paul, Trench & Co., 1887); *The Complete Poetical Works* (London, Bickers & Son, 1894).

Nesbit, Edith, *Lays and Legends* (London, Longmans, Green & Co., 1886); *A Pomander of Verses* (London, John Lane, 1895).

Caroline E. S. Norton, *The Undying One and Other Poems*, 2nd edition (London, Henry Colburn & Richard Bentley, 1830); *The Dream and Other Poems* (London, Henry Colburn, 1844).

O'Neill, Moira, *Songs of the Glens of Antrim* (Edinburgh, William Blackwood & Sons, 1900).

Procter, Adelaide Ann, *Legends and Lyrics*, 3rd edition (London, Bell & Daldy, 1859); *Poems*, Charles Dickens (intr.) (London, George Bell & Sons, 1882).

Radford, Dollie, *Songs and Other Verses* (London, The Bodley Head, 1895).

Robinson, Agnes Mary, *Songs, Ballads, and a Garden Play* (London, T. Fisher Unwin, 1888); *Retrospect and Other Poems* (London, T. Fisher Unwin, 1893).

Rossetti, Christina, *The Complete Poems*, Vols I & II, Variorum Edition, Rebecca W. Crump (ed.) (USA, Louisiana State University Press, 1979); *The Complete Poems*, W. M. Rossetti (ed.) (London, Macmillan & Co., 1904).

Sigerson, Dora, *Ballads and Poems* (London, James Bowden, 1899).

Veley, Margaret, *A Marriage of Shadows and other Poems*, Leslie Stephens (ed.) (London, Smith, Elder & Co., 1888).

Webster Augusta, *Blanche Lisle and Other Poems* (Cambridge, Macmillan & Co., 1860); *Lilian Gray: A Poem* (London, Smith Elder & Co., 1864); *Dramatic Studies* (London, Macmillan & Co., 1866); *A Woman Sold and Other Poems* (London, Macmillan & Co., 1867);

Portraits (London, Macmillan & Co., 1870); *The Sentence: A Drama* (London, T. Fisher Unwin, 1887); *A Book of Rhyme* (London, Macmillan & Co., 1881; *Mother and Daughter, An Uncompleted Sonnet Sequence*, W. M. Rossetti (intr.) (London, Macmillan & Co., 1895).

Woods, Margaret L., *Lyrics and Ballads* (London, Richard Bentley & Sons, 1889); *Aeromancy and Other Poems* (London, Elkin Mathews, 1896).

CHECKLISTS AND DICTIONARIES

Alston, R. C., *A Checklist of Women Writers, 1801–1900: Fiction, Verse, Drama* (London, The British Library, 1990).

Blain, Virginia, Clements, Patricia and Grundy, Isobel (eds), *The Feminist Companion to Literature in English: Women Writers from the Middle Ages to the Present* (London, B. T. Batsford, 1990).

Brady, Anne M. and Cleeve, Brian (eds), *A Biographical Dictionary of Irish Writers* (Dublin, The Lilliput Press, 1985).

Dictionary of National Biography, (O.U.P.)

Hammond, N. G. L. and Scullard, H. H. (eds), *The Oxford Classical Dictionary* (Oxford University Press, 1970, reprinted 1979).

O'Donoghue, D. J. (ed.), *The Poets of Ireland: A Biographical and Bibliographical Dictionary of Irish Writers of English Verse* (Dublin, Hodges Figgis & Co., reprinted Johnson Reprint Corporation, 1970).

Rose, H. J., *A Handbook of Greek Mythology* (London, Methuen, 1928, 6th edition, 1958, reprinted 1960).

Thorne, J. O. and T. L. Collocott (eds), *Chambers Biographical Dictionary* (Edinburgh, Chambers, revised 1984).

Todd, Janet (ed.), *A Dictionary of Women Writers* (London, Routledge, 1989).

Warrack, Alexander (comp.), *Chambers Scots Dictionary* (Edinburgh, W. & R. Chambers, 1911, reprinted 1968).

BIOGRAPHIES, MEMOIRS, ESSAYS, CRITICISM, SOCIAL HISTORY

Badeni, June, *The Slender Tree: A Life of Alice Meynell* (Cornwall, Tabb House, 1981).

Berridge, Elizabeth (sel. and intr.), *The Barretts at Hope End: the Early Diary of Elizabeth Barrett Browning* (London, John Murray, 1974).

Braybon, Gail and Summerfield, Penny, *Out of the Cage: Women's Experiences in Two World Wars* (London, Routledge, 1987).

Briggs, Julia, *A Woman of Passion: The Life of E. Nesbit 1858–1924* (London, Hutchinson, 1987).

Bristow, Joseph (ed.), *The Victorian Poet: Poetics and Persona* (Kent, Croom Helm, 1987).

Chedzoy, Alan, *A Scandalous Woman: The Story of Caroline Norton* (London, Allison & Busby, 1992).

Chitham, Edward, *A Life of Emily Brontë* (Oxford, Basil Blackwell, 1987).

Dennis, Barbara and Skilton, David (eds), *Reform and Intellectual Debate in Victorian England* (Kent, Croom Helm, 1987).

Evans, B. Ifor, *English Poetry in the Later Nineteenth Century* (London, Methuen, 1933, revised 1966).

Faderman, Lillian, *Surpassing the Love of Men* (USA, William Morrow & Co., 1981; London, Junction Books, 1982; London, The Women's Press, 1985).

Feather, John, *A History of British Publishing* (London, Routledge, 1988).

Gilbert, Sandra and Gubar, Susan (eds), *The Madwoman in the Attic: The Woman Writer and the Nineteenth-Century Imagination* (New Haven and London, Yale University Press, 1979).

Hayter, Alethea, *Elizabeth Barrett Browning*, 'Writers and Their Work Series' (London, Longmans, Green & Co., 1965).

Hickok, Kathleen, *Representations of Women: Nineteenth-Century British Women's Poetry* (Westport, Connecticut, Greenswood Press, 1984).

Homans, Margaret, *Women Writers and Poetic Identity: Dorothy Wordsworth, Emily Brontë, and Emily Dickinson* (Princeton University Press, 1980).

Hughes, William R., *Constance Naden: A Memoir* (London, Bickers & Son, 1890).

Karlin, Daniel, (sel. and ed.), *Robert Browning and Elizabeth Barrett: The Courtship Correspondence 1845–46* (Oxford University Press, 1989).

Lane, Maggie, *Literary Daughters* (London, Robert Hale, 1989).

Lane, Margaret, *The Brontë Story: A Reconsideration of Mrs Gaskell's Life of Charlotte Brontë* (London, Heinemann, 1953, reprinted 1966).

Leighton, Angela, *Victorian Women Poets: Writing Against the Heart* (Brighton, Harvester, 1992).

Marshall, Dorothy, *Fanny Kemble* (London, Weidenfeld & Nicolson, 1977).

Mermin, Dorothy, *Elizabeth Barrett Browning: The Origins of a New Poetry* (University of Chicago Press, 1989).

Meynell, Viola, *Alice Meynell: A Memoir* (London, Jonathan Cape, 1929).

Montefiore, Jan, *Feminism and Poetry: Language, Experience, Identity In Women's Writing* (London, Pandora, Routledge, 1987).

Nunn, Pamela Gerrish, *Victorian Women Artists* (London, The Women's Press, 1987).

Peters, Margo, *Unquiet Soul: A Biography of Charlotte Brontë* (London, Hodder & Stoughton, 1975).

Packer, Lona Mosk, *Christina Rossetti* (University of California Press; Cambridge University Press, 1963).

Showalter, Elaine, *The New Feminist Criticism: Essays on Women, Literature and Theory* (New York, Pantheon, 1985; London, Virago, 1986).

Swindells, Julia, *Victorian Writing and Working Women: The Other Side of Silence* (London, Polity Press, 1985).

Vicinus, Martha, *The Industrial Muse: A Study of Nineteenth-Century British Working-Class Literature* (London, Croom Helm, 1974); *A Widening Sphere: Changing Roles of Victorian Women* (Indiana University Press, 1977; London, Methuen & Co., 1980); *Independent Women: Work and Community for Single Women* (University of Chicago Press, Virago Press, 1985).

Winnifrith, Tom, *The Brontës* (New York, Collier Macmillan, 1977).

INDEX OF AUTHORS

INDEX OF FIRST LINES AND TITLES